Traveling

An Accidental Expert's How To Leave Your Body Handbook

Alan Guiden

First published 2009
by Aeon Books Ltd.
London W5
www.aeonbooks.co.uk

British Library Cataloging in Publication Data
A C.I.P. is available for this book from the British Library.

ISBN-13: 978-1-90465-833-7

A Brief History of Me

- ➤ I had my first conscious out of body 'travel' when I was eight.

- ➤ In the years that followed I searched for the out of body answers while I lived the questions.

- ➤ My trial-and-error years of experience made me an accidental expert.

- ➤ It has become my responsibility to share what I've learned.

THE PRESENT

My informal how-to 'travel' book will provide you with the previously scattered and absent answers to the questions of leaving your body. All of the important nonphysical information is here.

You may believe that the out of body experience is just a delightful dream. I welcome that notion. I'll be speaking specifically about my knowledge of being 'out' and will address how 'nonphysical' feels and behaves, but this doesn't dictate that you must buy into my conclusions. Try some of the suggestions and formulate an opinion that's correct for you. Enjoy the scenery. Interesting discoveries will be yours regardless of your direction.

I'm sure you've heard about out of body experiences before. You may have heard slanted, angled, lopsided, believe-it-this-way-or-that explanations. Well, we'll have none of that here. Sit back and get comfortable. I'll fill you in on my story and, if you feel like it, you'll soon have your own to tell.

Alan Guiden

Contents

MY FIRST TRAVELS

I was an average child living an average life until sometime during my eighth year. After that point I was an average child living *two* lives. The second life was beyond my comprehension or ability to control. Waking up in that life was a terrifying attraction.

If you've read my short opening statements, before you arrived at this page, you'll know a little of my past. But if you bypassed that part you'd best go back and read it now, or you'll fall behind. Meanwhile, I'll tell you of a typical night's adventure when I was a child. You can read it when you get back.

AGE EIGHT

It was just before dawn when I awoke to find myself on the floor of my pitch-dark room. I was concerned that I couldn't recall the apparent fall from my bed and I began to flail in the dark for signs of the familiar. It was as if I was grasping at water. My short unsuccessful search elevated childish concern to a panic. In desperation, I screamed for my mother. It was a strong scream, the most powerful of my life. It was also the most silent. Immediately, I shot back into my bed like a rocket. I was still screaming but there wasn't any voice. My fear was locked behind frozen lips. My body beneath the covers was paralyzed. An electric deafening roar rumbled through me. It shook my body with a violent grip. And then, it suddenly subsided. The vibrational roar eased off and my catatonic state simply faded away. Movement returned to my body. I was back.

Disclaimers To You

There are no long-term side effects to 'traveling' out of your body, aside perhaps from an obsession to understand this strange phenomenon. Of the possible short term side effects, most of them are fun.

Soapbox

I hate professional jargon. I'm referring to the numerous buzzwords and phrases that can clutter an otherwise understandable conversation. Jargon-junk makes it that much more difficult to grasp the concepts being presented.

In this book, I'll be fixing the out of body dictionary. I'll use only easy words and phrases that fit the concept, and I'll be denoting them 'like so', while you get the hang of thinking 'nonphysically'. You may have caught on already that I've been denoting since the start of this book. If so, you have a good eye for detail and will make an excellent 'traveler'. In understanding that this book is about 'getting out' you will soon have a full grasp of how to do it without all the confusing claptrap.

A good example of my out of body dictionary is the word, 'traveling'. That's mine. When I realized years ago that I should share my work, I chose that jargon-free word because it describes exactly what you're doing when you're doing it. You are 'traveling nonphysically'. You could be anywhere, from your bedroom to another town or on the moon. And although your bedroom is not far away, you'll soon learn that even a short jaunt is a 'nonphysical travel' you'll be proud of. Too bad you can't take along a camera.

Table Of Our Contents

I'm just some guy with an odd talent. In the beginning my 'travels' just happened on their own. I was an unwitting subject. After many years of 'traveling' I've figured out how it works and how it sometimes doesn't work. Learning to 'travel' doesn't require you to believe any differently from how you do now. You can be any type of person, with any background, and still find what works most of the time. You assemble your specific combination of 'pieces', which results in a nonphysical travel for you, the individual.

Me And More Me

As a result of years of research conducted upon me by me it appears to me that there are Seven Steps that make up an out of body 'travel'. And if this is true for me, and all my mes' seem to agree, then likely this is true for you too. Me has an abundance of experience and knowledge on which to speak and me is therefore correct in this instance.

Your Travel Options

1. Ignore the following and also the previous.
2. Answer your phone, whether it is ringing or not, and say that you're too busy not paying attention to be bothered.
3. Shake your head in vigorous disagreement to this sentence.
4. Sit in the corner. Stop fidgeting.
5. Try to see things my way, then your way, then the way a dog might see things—and lastly, a parrot.
6. Write your name on a cereal box.
7. Dance a jig.
8. Look at the sky then the ground then the sky then the ground then the sky. Hey, you're a bobble-head!
9. Read some more of this book.
10. Keep an open mind and see where it leads you.

The First Year

Following my initially terrifying introduction to 'traveling' were more events of a similar nature. Going to bed became a contradiction in terms. It became a routine of the unknown. I was never sure where I'd 'wake up' while out of body. I 'woke up' in the neighbor's house. I woke up at my elementary school. I woke up in the woods at the end of the block. I woke in every place of which a child's world consists.

During my early travels my realization of what was happening arrived slowly, as if through a haze. I'd fumble around trying to discern objects that might be familiar, like a wall or a doorway. I was drawn to my neighbor's house because I had been there before. I was the same age as their daughter who went to my school, and our parents hung out together. It was the usual set of reasons a child has for being anywhere. When I 'awoke' in their house, it was additionally confusing because their tract-house was designed to be exactly the opposite of my house. Like looking in a mirror, I'd turn left to enter a room and 'run into' a wall instead. It only become clear that I was in their house when I stumbled across one of our wacky neighbor's vinyl-wrapped chairs. The vinyl was to protect the furniture from children and was removed for dinner parties and martini lunches. When I 'fell' over the chair I immediately knew where I was. And with this recognition of 'where' came clarity. I began to understand that I was not sleeping but I was not awake. I was moving and aware but I wasn't in my body. It was not a dream. I was really in my neighbor's house. My early travels were like this, a slow realization of my surroundings, and then 'focus'.

The 'return' to bed was especially frightening when I first began traveling. I'd be enjoying a pleasant nonphysical stroll in the front yard when suddenly I'd be jerked back to my paralyzed physical body and a 'vibrating' roar that engulfed all of my senses. I was isolated from any outside events, often for more than a half hour. If the phone rang or lightning had struck, I'd never have known nor been capable of reacting.

Coping with the 'return' was difficult until I came to realize that it was happening whether I wanted it to or not. My only option was to maintain a patient, inquisitive attitude. After I had experienced the gripping 'vibration' many times I learned that it eventually faded away and that I'd be all right when it left. I became determined to do nothing. I would not struggle against it. I would discover what I could while the 'vibration' was present. It was a matter of forcing myself to remain as calm as possible during the storm.

From eight to nine years old I was 'traveling' all the time. Although I still didn't grasp what the event was, I did learn what to expect. I began to think of the 'travels' as normal for me but I rarely spoke of them with family or friends. I was always disappointed by their response to my exciting tale of the 'real dream' from the night before. I had hoped for answers or similar stories but this quirky adventure seemed to be my game alone.

A MEMORY OF ME

I'm on my back, lying on my bed. My eyelids are shut tight. My arms and legs are locked. Nothing will move. I can't hear anything above the roar. It keeps happening. But it doesn't hurt. It's just shaking me. If I don't force myself to move I'll learn what this is. I want to understand how this works.

THE BIG WRAP UP

At the age of twelve I found a metaphysical book at the library that had a chapter about something called "astral projection". While I don't care for that phrase today, at the time it was magic. I couldn't believe what I was reading. There were others like myself. My excitement was boundless because I wasn't alone. Since the Internet was years away from becoming what it is today, I began to search for tidbits of "astral" information in bookstores and magazines. While it was comforting to read about the topic, it didn't take long before it occurred to me that most of it was fluff and reruns. I knew more about 'traveling' than I was reading. It was the impact of this realization that pushed my silent study beyond a curious fascination. The answers had become my responsibility.

SEVEN STEPS

You've been very patient while I prattled on about my childhood and here's your reward. You're about to learn how to get out of your physical body, *and* I shall keep on prattling. Oh lucky you.

There are *Seven Steps* to intentionally traveling out of body.

1. Desire
2. Relaxation
3. Visualization and Destination
4. Direct Lift-out
5. Awareness
6. Travel
7. Return and Memory

Each step is an important singular piece and also important as a whole. Your subconscious thoughts and a variety of physical factors also play a part. We'll get to those soon, don't rush me.

To introduce briefly the Seven Steps here's a quick, not so random event from when I was ten. I'll tell the story and then break it down into the steps. It'll be fun. I cross my fingers and promise it will. Although the following travel was completely unintentional it was propelled by the same seven steps you'll be using.

At age ten I was fond of gymnastics. My favorite activity was tumbling end over end down a long mat like a ridiculous circus clown.

My craving for tumbling also manifested itself during my restful hours. At night, in my focused thoughts, I'd envision the rolling and leaping. Over and over I'd jump and roll and jump and roll and jump and... It was quite by accident from my mental-tumbling that I discovered an ability for pushing my nonphysical out of the top of my head. Although it was incredibly fun, it was also disconcerting as I actually felt as if I were flinging my entire physical body forward, up and out of the bed to crash into the wall. From there the shock of being 'out' immediately dragged me right back into my physical.

Now I'll break down the experience into the seven steps:

1. Desire
I wanted to tumble. I focused on tumbling. I did tumble, nonphysically.

2. Relaxation
Although I had not intentionally 'controlled' my relaxation I was deeply relaxed while focused on tumbling.

3. Visualization — Destination

I visualized myself tumbling to satisfy my desire. A destination can be a person, place, object, or 'action'. The destination in this event was the 'action' of tumbling.

4. Direct Lift-Out

My nonphysical tumbled out as an 'uncontrolled' response to my focused desire. This puts the lift-out into the category of 'indirect' but who cares because it was a hoot.

5. Awareness

My awareness while out was excellent but totally 'uncontrolled' and exceedingly giddy.

6. Travel

The travel was a unintentional nonphysical head-first roll-out from the physical and a tumble across the room into a wall.

7. Return

The short travel was followed by an immediate return to the physical and lots of smiling. Nothing beats being 'out'.

Memory

A clean memory of the nonphysical event requires that it be imprinted upon the physical brain, immediately upon return. A simple conscious effort to recall the nonphysical event, after returning to the physical, is enough to imprint the travel. If the return to the physical is followed instead by falling directly to sleep, without committing the event from nonphysical knowledge to physical knowledge, there's a good chance of a muddled memory later or none at all of the event.

Thankfully, so that I could tell you my oh-so-fascinating tumbling story today, my amusement during the event created an immediate imprint on my physical and I carry a vivid memory. But I don't know where I've left my car keys.

Step One: Desire

You Want It

Most early travels are 'unintentional'. They are subconsciously motivated by desire and *poof* you're out. As you've read, my tumble from bed followed the basic principle that drives both the 'subconscious unintentional' travel and the 'conscious intentional' travel. The principle is *desire*. I'm tired of the word 'tumble' now.

Desire is the first step, the real oomph pushing the 'nonphysical travel'. For instance, if I ask you to go over and pick up that penny, you have a few choices. You can choose to pick up the penny; you can choose not to pick up the penny; or you can choose not to believe there is a penny. Regardless of your choice, I've tricked you into visualizing the penny, even if you think there is none, which is important and we'll get to that soon. We're not in a hurry. Well, at least I'm not. If you have things to do, stop back later. And bring me some nachos.

To continue, if you chose not to pick up the penny or chose not to believe it exists, then you're no fun at all. But, nonphysically speaking, if you chose to pick up the penny, that becomes your 'desire' that triggers your 'action' that becomes your 'destination' and so you travel from your body to fulfill your desire. It's a happy circle that brings you what you desire. *Weeeeeeee.*

As you can see, even a simple desired 'action' like picking up a penny can 'trigger your travel'. Say that three times fast. But what if the penny meant a lot to you? What if you and that penny had been through some good times together? That penny and you are the best of friends. So now, instead of going to pick up the penny as an 'action', your bond with your beloved penny aims you like an arrow of desire. You want to be with penny. Penny means everything to you. Penny is calling you. Off you go!

That's one example of 'ramping up' your desire to reach your 'destination'. You simply 'focus' your emotional bond with a person, place, object, or action, and allow yourself to go to it or do it.

Instead of penny you could've used a loved one as your 'desired destination'. It's been so long since you've seen (insert a name of someone you can tolerate here). It sure would be good to see them again. Remember all the fabulous times (make up some lies) that (insert name again) and you used to share. You really want to be there with them. You're so looking forward to being there. Off you go.

That's another example of ramping up an emotional desire that 'pushes' you from your physical body. But maybe you don't like anybody. Maybe you'd rather be alone at that creek by your house where it's nice and quiet and water rushes by and trees sway and there are birds and tadpoles and it smells so fresh just hanging out by the creek. Off you go.

That's the final example of ramping up an emotional desire, until I change my mind and write more later. I think you get the concept, but I'll repeat it anyway. You take your strong emotional desire for a person, place, object, or action, and you focus on the bond that connects you. You *want* to be there. You *want* to go now. Off you go.

FOCUS AND DESIRE

Any emotion may be used as a 'focus' to keep you 'alert' until you're ready to get out of your body. Happy emotions include joy and love. Unhappy emotions include anger and fear. Anything that you feel in your day-to-day life may be used as a 'focus'. The happy emotions are usually more pleasant to use as a 'focus' but the unhappy emotions can be useful and fulfilling as well, if kept in check.

Another instance from my experience, since I'm the only one typing here: I hate-hate-hated working at this store in my past. The store was a combination glass bricabrac and jewelry shop. The work was sooooo boring and inane. After work, while home in my bed, I'd ponder the last wretched eight hours. I'd 'focus' on letting it all go in the best way possible: I wrecked the place in my thoughts. The store never stood a chance. Although I would never do this in my real life, as I'm the non-violent type, I would trash a few things while relaxing in bed. You can too and it's a lot of fun.

You may utilize your anger and aggression as a 'focus'. This intense 'focus' keeps you 'alert' as you drift off towards physical sleep. By being 'alert', while your body sleeps, your chances of achieving a conscious travel greatly increase. Another benefit of this method is the release of the unhappy emotion. Like a primal scream, the volume of your anger will relieve you of stress. You simply focus on the emotion until your physical is snoozing. Then you let go of the emotions and re-focus on your traveling 'plan'.

For example, I'd imagine smashing the displays in the empty store with a baseball bat. Glass shattered and soared from the blows. I'll get you, hand-crafted glass ashtray! Take that, silver necklace trinkets! I'd run around the store smashing and thrashing. Nothing was safe from my baseball bat. And then I'd hear myself snore. During my focused frenzy my physical was being ignored and did what it was supposed to do, it fell asleep. The snoring was my 'signal' to now re-focus on my 'desire' and go traveling.

When you use an 'emotional focus' as a method to leave your body your 'imagery' will be all encompassing. It will exclude other thoughts. It will center you. You will be in that moment of emotion and release. And then POW!, you'll realize that your physical body is sleeping while you are completely awake and alert. It may be that you hear yourself snore while using an emotional focus or any number of other 'signals'. As I'll explain soon, you have time to make a cup of tea, these 'signals' will alert you that your body in bed doesn't give a care if you venture out for a while.

As we're here anyway, I'll give a brief example of a focused emotion that scares you into staying alert while your physical sleeps. I was going to present a happy emotion as the example here, but I figure you can imagine little bunnies hopping around a flower garden without my help. Instead, I'll talk about sharks.

I love man-eating sharks. They are just so cool with their skills and teeth. I studied them quite a bit following that movie that scared everyone out of the water. They are fascinating creatures. And if I were ever to be stranded, clutching that big toilet-looking ring out in the ocean, I would be scared beyond words. I just know I'm going to be mistaken for a seal or floppy fish.

This method of emotional focus works almost too well. What we are afraid of creates an intense imagery. You simply allow yourself to get sucked into that vortex of fright, if you can handle it. You take the ride until your physical falls asleep, and then you re-focus on your desire and it pulls you from your body.

The water is so dark. All I can see is the ocean's surface reflecting starlight and wave caps. I wish I'd remembered to put that five dollar plug back in the bottom of the boat. Hey, what was that?! A ripple in the water just moved past, twelve feet long at least. Ack, there's another one! Something nudged me, I just felt it! Oh, this is *it*. I'm creeping myself out. I have to stop.

During the shark imagery my physical would quickly drift off to sleep. When I could no longer take the scariness I'd break myself free of the fright by recognizing that it was not real. I'd then re-focus on a desire to be above the water, flying over the moonlit ocean nearest my home. Because I was completely alert I was instantly pulled from my physical and speeding past the houses hundreds of feet below. I arrived at the ocean in a few seconds. I moved closer to the rolling surface. To be there, unsupported above all that water, is an experience not to be forgotten. You really must try it. And the sharks look so cute and cuddly from up there. You can't hurt me! Oh sure, a shark might scare me if they took a physical snap at my nonphysical body, but there's no damage done. Except that you'd call me Fishbait from now on. That would be rude.

Your first attempt at an emotional focus might be somewhat closer to home and less adventurous than shark-infested waters. Those little bunnies hopping around a flower garden, for instance.

Dear Diary

Hello friendly reader. Please pay attention to your night time activity by writing it down. Simply write a few sentences that describe in minor detail the 'events' you recall. Even if your 'event' doesn't seem nonphysical, write it down. Then date it and put it under your pillow. I'm kidding. Don't do that very last bit. But do all the rest of what I said, like so:

September 22
Last night I accidentally scared a cat that was lounging in the yard near the bird baths. I then watched as my neighbor arrived home late from somewhere and fell out of his car. And lastly, I zoomed past my bedroom window and ran into a tree. Another eventful night.

You can see how great 'event' diaries can be and why you should keep one. And now that I've talked you into it, I should tell you that I hate writing in a diary. Oh my, it's boring. But I did it anyway from about the age of ten. I started writing in one of those blank diaries sold to kids. My first one was a manly blue diary so stop making fun of me. These days I keep a small voice recorder near the bed and mumble into it, on 'return' from wherever I just was. I call this a lazy-diary and it works just as well as writing things down. So do either one and make me happy.

The point of keeping a diary is to pay attention pay attention. Yes, I typed that twice. It's very good of you to pay attention. Do I have your attention? Then let's move on. Pay attention to the small details of your 'events' and put them in your diary. You may notice, as an instance of paying attention, that I have avoided using the word "dream" and have replaced that word with 'event'. Your event may be a dream in your physical or a dream 'acted' outside of your physical. Your event may occur while you are semiconscious or unconscious. Your event may be a fully conscious nonphysical travel. You can learn from all of your 'events' to improve your chances at traveling the next time.

It is your attitude, focused upon the desire to re-call your events, that helps you to do so. It is your unbridled wish to ponder this previously unpon-dered state that allows you to see it clearly. It is your intentional intensity of attention that en-hances your ability to grasp what you are up to while your physical sleeps!

So if you scared a cat near the birdbath or zoomed past your window, Pay Attention. And when you watch from above as your neighbor pours out of his car at 2am, Pay Attention. You may be in your body and dreaming or out of your body and dreaming. You may be traveling semi-consciously. Your attention to the event will 'wake you up'. Paying attention to the 'details' of your event will also help you to improve your out of body skills. I'll get to those later, so mellow out.

You Score

As you've read (if you weren't skipping chapters willy nilly) your desire is the force pushing the travel. It is such a strong force in fact that you can use desire, which is step one of seven, without having any working knowledge of the other steps at all! How's that for getting right to the point?

Tonight, in your bed or futon or dresser drawer or whatever you sleep on, think of an emotional 'goal'. A 'goal' includes an 'action' you take that is pushed by desire, resulting in what you set out to do.

For instance, your emotional 'goal' might be to visit your sweetie two towns over. You desire to be there. You focus on your 'action' which, in this case, is the route you plan to travel as your physical relaxes down to sleep. You'll go out your window, down the block, up a few hundred feet, 'home' in on your wittle whoosy woowoo, and rocket your way there. Pet names are so embarrassing.

The emotional goal is just one type of 'goal' you might set for yourself. Your goal might be 'inquisitive', a desire to learn something. You might wish to see what's on the other side of that hill, or take a gander at your neighbor's new rider mower, or you might want to visit a place that you've read about. Although there is an emotional aspect present, in wanting to learn something through these goals, they are more 'action' motivated. Your desire pushes you forward in action towards your goal of knowing this or that.

Another type of goal is 'experience'. You want to achieve something, to do it and feel it. You want to leave your house by walking through the front door. You want to float out over your porch and look up in the night sky. You want to blast off at full throttle, up up up up. Your goal is to 'experience' being there thousands of feet above your house. Your goal is fueled by desire, which initiates the action, so that you get what you want. And who deserves it more than you?

As you see, you can use desire and a goal without really knowing anything more of what I plan to tell you. You could just take a week or so of nighttimes and give this streamlined version of traveling a try. It's simple and almost always brings interesting results. It's also a good jumping-off point for learning the other six steps, whether you want to know about them or not.

Ten To Seventeen

My years from ten to seventeen were probably like yours. I was facing the usual demands that most kids encounter. I handled the pressures. I wasn't the most popular nor the least. I was just average with an unusual hobby.

My out of body travels were in full force. I traveled occasionally by choice and constantly by whim on an average of at least once a day. The unintentional travels brought me to places I hadn't planned to go, but later I could rationalize why I had gone there. The intentional travels could be frustrating since a method I used might work one time but not the next. This turned out to be a good learning experience, as I'll explain on another page when I get there. *Another page,* I said. Stop looking here for the reason. Stop it. I *mean* it. I'm just going to move on, then. You can keep looking here if you want but you're wasting your time.

STEP TWO: RELAXATION

Zzz

Who are you kidding, laying there in your bed? You'll never relax. But wait, perhaps I typed too soon. You *are* feeling kind of relaxed now. Yeah, this might be it. There you go. Relaxing. Relaxing. Alright, you're really relaxed. Now just stay alert. Relax and stay alert. You can do it, relax but stay... ZZZzzzzzzzz.

Huh, what? Oh, hi again. You were looking so relaxed there you made me fall asleep. But I can't blame you for all the times I fell asleep during my search for nonphysical answers. It's not that I was sleepy. I simply went a little too far into my work. Or that's what I tell myself.

I would try to relax, to let my body sleep, while I would stay alert and focused on traveling. I'm relaxing now. Down and down. I'm relaxing and staying focused on my traveling 'plan'. Focused on my... ZZZzzzzzzzz.

Dagnabit, I fell asleep again. I'm clearly going to have a hard time finishing this section. But let's press on anyway and tour the 'awake/asleep line' while we're here.

The Awake/Asleep Line

The 'awake/asleep line' is a key element of traveling. It's the line between losing consciousness and falling into sleep, as your physical body does, or remaining awake, alert and in control while your physical body falls to sleep. To reach the line you simply regulate your movement towards sleep. *Simply?* Haha, what am I saying? Because, just as you bargain for that last moment of rest before having to get up in the morning, when you are close to the awake/asleep line, it's all too tempting to just drift over that thin line into sweet sleep. But if you do that you'll never control a travel. So put that out of your mind this instant. Forget that I brought up that beautiful, tranquil sleep that is just on the other side of the line. There it is. Oh sleep sleep sleep.

Now really, you've *got* to stay awake. The temptation of crossing the line into sleep is great but can be overcome some of the time with 'controlled relaxation' methods. Controlled relaxation allows you to stay alert some of the time while your physical body relaxes down into sleep. And why do I keep saying "some of the time"? Because during your search for good relaxation methods, that work for you some of the time, you are going to fall asleep.

To prepare for the awake/asleep line, you choose a relaxation method and a travel 'plan'.

Your relaxation method drops you down near to physical sleep while you remain alert. You then step onto the line, allowing your physical to take the final plunge into sleep. When it does, you maintain your control and transfer your consciousness from your sleeping physical body to your willing nonphysical body. You 'push' yourself into your travel plan and off you go. Some of the time.

RELAX ALREADY

As you explore the nature of traveling there will be times when you suddenly 'awaken' right on the awake/asleep line in stunned but confident control. It's what you've been training for and—surprise—here it is. Thankfully you're prepared, because you thought ahead about this happening when you read it in some handbook you bought.

There, on the line, you can feel your nonphysical body. Your nonphysical isn't sleeping but your physical is. You are fully conscious and in control. And because your physical is slumbering and your nonphysical is willing and your travel plan is ready and your desire is strong, off you go. Some of the time.

More often than not you will have to work your way down to the awake/asleep line, not just find yourself there. So it's a good thing I have some methods and tricks that help you remain alert while relaxing your physical. Be sure to visit a library, or surf the internet too, for other relaxation methods to keep your traveling fresh and exciting. There is no shortage of relaxation methods designed to calm us *all* down. We're all too jumpy! We've got to mellow out! Stop climbing around. I mean it—come down from there! That's it, no more energy drinks for you. You need to calm down so that we can work our way to the awake/asleep line. Then we'll get you set up with some travel plans and delve into the nifty things that happen when you're nonphysical. It'll all be just spectacular, I promise. Some of the time.

Recording Relaxation

Testing. Testing, one, two. This is a test of the *Get Out Of Your Body Testing System*. If you are hearing this recording within the confines of your physical body it's because earlier today you recorded some positive and calming thoughts into a recording device and now they are playing back to you while you lay upon your bed. "I am so relaxed and at ease", the recording of your voice says. "I am relaxed and comfortable. It's so quiet and peaceful. My body feels so light and relaxed. I am alert and relaxed. I am aware and relaxed. I am relaxed and in control." This concludes this test of the testing system being tested for this test.

As relaxation methods go, recording your voice and then playing it back is one of the best. Nothing beats hearing your own voice tell you to do things that you want to do anyway. You can customize the words that relax you, while keeping you focused and alert. You can set a traveling plan in your thoughts or inspire a dream you want to have or just talk yourself to sleep. You can make different recordings for what you want on specific nights. It's the power of your own voice, and the exact nature of your words, that has an effect unmatched by many methods.

I am currently using a twenty-dollar digital recording device I bought from a large chain store. It stores three hundred minutes, which is more than enough for you to record some words to yourself about being relaxed and in control as you travel out of your body. You can borrow it. Or you could wander over to that heap you're calling a closet and see if you already have a recording device in there. I think it's in a shoe box. Once you've found it go find a piece of paper. I think I saw some in the kitchen. Write a script to record, which includes words you find pleasing and relaxing. Include suggestions to remain alert and aware as your physical drifts towards sleep.

Even at this early point, before I have explained many out of body traveling tricks, you can add a simple traveling plan to your recordings. You can insert a few words throughout your recording with a small 'action' involved: "I will take an out of body stroll to the garden"; "I will explore the ceiling in the hallway"; "I will sneak up on the cat, *as if* I can". Once your script is complete find a quiet place to hide from everyone who might think you're talking to yourself and make your recording. If you have the ability to loop the recording, all the better. Try to give yourself at least fifteen minutes of you talking to yourself. Repeating the same script over and over is fine and actually desirable for this method.

An added bonus to this method is the ability to set a timer for the playback of the recording. Set your timer to go off after you've had a few hours sleep. Set the volume of playback to gently rouse you from slumber. Since your physical is already relaxed it takes less effort to convince it to fall asleep again. And, with your consciousness sharp from a bit of down time, this is perfect for your out of body intentions.

You can replay your recordings anytime, except when operating a motor vehicle or using heavy equipment. So I'll just wait for you to put down the sofa with that forklift. It was fine over there by the window anyway. You should listen to your recordings when you feel they'll work the best for you. Maybe you have a spare hour on Sunday morning or some time just before you go to sleep at night or some time a few hours after you sleep or just because you're laying in bed not sleeping anyway. The more you hear your recording the better it works. You may find the suggestions of your recording occurring even when you're not playing it back. That's because your words to yourself are in your subconscious and conscious thoughts now and you can't get them out. This is usually a good thing unless you told yourself to think you're a goose whenever the doorbell rings.

If you're hearing impaired, not to worry. This is just one method of many. You could still write a few scripts and commit them to memory. Then, when you're ready to relax, recall your script as best as possible. Focus on your plan to stay alert as you relax. Think about your travel. Off you go.

Another Memory Of Me

I was an oddball grandson. I was fourteen when I visited with my grandparents in Florida. Since they took naps every afternoon I decided I'd use that time to play back the recordings I had brought with me for the trip. The recordings I made at that time were very specifically honed to deepen my relaxation and follow though with a travel plan. The elders would grumble off to their bed-chambers and I'd lay on the carpeted floor, which I was into at that time, with a pillow. The less than familiar surroundings, combined with the less than comfortable laying about on the floor, combined with the more than merely unusual recordings, worked amazingly well. Oh how the grandparents slept while I nonphysically wandered around their condo and down to their little man-made lake and over to the spot where they re-charged the golf carts that they drove everywhere, including the store. Their age-gated community was my out of body playground. Granny and Gramps go to bed and I leap out of my body. I was an oddball then and I'm still waiting to grow out of that phase.

Seeing Is Believing

I see you there reading these words. There you are. I see as your eyes move across the letters on the page. I see you wondering what I'm up to next and why can't I just get to it. I see you trying to figure out what I'm teaching you by introducing this chapter the way that I am. I see you looking over to the coffee table with one leg shorter than the others. I see you taking this book over to balance the table. I see it's dusty down here under the table. You should clean more often. I see you walking away to the kitchen. Fine. I'll just sit here in the dust under the table and 'visualize' all by myself.

'Visualization' works just as well as any recorded suggestions you might have made of your voice that you play back over and over and over and let me know when you get tired of reading over and over and you should be getting close now over and over and come on already I'm getting carpal tunnel over and over and over and anytime you want to stop it will probably stop over and over and over. Nicely done.

You just visualized an ending to that ridiculous paragraph and there it was. You are really starting to get the hang of this whole visualization thing and I've yet to formally introduce the topic. Actually, we're so far along now that I don't see a need to do that anyway. Instead, here is a basic 'visualization' that relaxes your body in bed yet keeps you focused and alert, which improves your chances of traveling out of your body:

A. You're at the top of a ladder. Stop reading, I don't want you to fall. Badabing. You're at the top of a long ladder.

B. Step down the ladder.

C. As you venture down your ladder, think about how relaxed and alert you're becoming. You're so relaxed, moving down and down. Step by step, relaxing deeply as you move further and further. You're alert and relaxing. When you reach the bottom you know that you'll be completely relaxed and alert. Down and down you go. No rush, as you go down and down your ladder to relaxation and alertness. You're at the bottom. You're comfortably relaxed and alert.

To further advance your visualization towards getting out of your body, include a traveling plan. See in your thoughts what you'd like to do or accomplish while you're traveling out of your body. Desire to be someplace close-by and see yourself go there. There's your living room with the comfortable chair and the television. The popcorn and precious ale call to you from the coffee table with a handbook balancing out that uneven leg. You see yourself sit up in your bed. You move to the doorway. You go down the hall. You sneak up on the cat, *as if* you can. You enter your living room. You move to the comfortable chair. It is then that you realize you can't eat popcorn or drink ale while nonphysical.

Visualization relaxes you and keeps you alert. Visualization is the route you take in your thoughts so you know where you're going. Visualization moves your focus away from your bedroom and allows your physical to toddle off to Snoreland. Then it's off you go to the living room just as you planned.

In addition to being an excellent way to get nonphysical, visualization will push annoying busy-thoughts away like a big friendly something or other that you might conjure up in your twisted mind.

Take A Vacation

You're on a raft in the middle of a soothing lake, floating under a clear blue sky. An ant swims by. He waves at you to attract your attention. He shouts from the water, "Hey dopey, stop thinking about ants! Try relaxing a bit," he says, "Think about how relaxing this lake is. Why, I don't think you could find a nicer, quieter or more relaxing lake than you have right here, by golly," the long-winded ant proclaims. The ant then grabs your bag of sandwiches from the raft and paddles quickly away using two carrot sticks as oars. Before long you hear the ant shout from across the lake, *"Stopppppppp thinkinggggg aboutttttt antsssssss!"*

Nothing relaxes you more than someplace relaxing. I wonder where you like to relax so that I can get in on your action. Your shower relaxes you, I bet. But I'm not going in there. How about your chair in the living room? That looks pretty relaxing. I could enjoy some serious relaxation there. And your hammock looks relaxing. I'll get in that and swing around for a relaxing hour. Do you like relaxing at the beach? I could borrow your lawn chair and your sunbrella and be very relaxed. Yes indeed. Comfortably lounging on a nice warm day down by the beach. The waves rolling in and out, the gulls calling from above the surf. A light breeze wafts the fresh ocean air. You are so relaxed. So relaxed in your special place. Oops, did I say *you*? I meant *me*. It's me here at your beach using your lawn chair and sunbrella and sipping your icy cold drink. Did I mention that I took your drink? Well, it's too late now, so get over it. But while I have you here in your special place, that can be any amazing place you have ever been or can imagine, let me tell you this. You can use your handy visualization to relax yourself into a place just like this beach.

While thinking of a pleasing place, you remain alert by observing the small details of what makes that place perfect for you. You run your hand through the sand, you hear the gulls singing, some klutz trips over your beach towel. You focus on these pleasing details while your physical moves to snooze. Then, when you consciously reach the awake/asleep line, you may either nonphysically visit a beach or have an alternate plan ready for a travel elsewhere or with a different agenda.

Skip This Part

I hate to bring this up, so just go right on past this chapter and don't feel guilty. Move on ahead. There's nothing you need to read here. Well, you had your chance. You could always do some light exercise before bedtime to tucker out your physical and sharpen your alertness. Of course, if you get lots of exercise in your daily routine this is not as important. But if you sit in your chair all day, as I am doing now, you could probably benefit from actual movement. On a doctor's okay, you could get up, move around, hop on one foot, dance the mambo, do aerobics, or just twiddle your thumbs. Doing an active bit of this or that prior to your relaxation method *du jour* will improve your chances of consciously reaching the awake/asleep line and traveling.

Once your body is worked a bit, get back into bed. Take a shower first if you wouldn't mind. Move into your relaxation method while staying alert. You'll find that your physical slides more quickly and easily towards sleep, so be ready to put your traveling plan into action when you're near the line. More on that is coming up but first get me a cup of coffee. No, wait. I just remembered the other thing I hated to bring up.

Better Make It Decaf

Here are some things we like to drink and eat: coffee and caffeinated tea and sodas and chocolaty candy bars and cookies. And here are some things that can really screw up a good relaxation method if consumed too close to your traveling attempt: coffee and caffeinated tea and sodas and chocolaty candy bars and cookies. Simply stated, as I'm the simpleton stating it, if you enjoy these goodies too late in the day a travel's less likely, so *hip hip hooray*! As you can see I'm hopped-up on coffee. Don't let this happen to you when you're trying to travel.

The other side of being too jumpy is being too relaxed due to over-consumption of alcohol or something else fun. Did I say *fun*? I meant *terribly fun*. No, I meant *terrible* and not fun at all. That's what I meant. The simpleton rule is don't do an overabundance of anything prior to your travel attempts. Your goal is to be relaxed but alert and in control for your visit to the awake/asleep line.

Some People Are Above Average But You're Not

As I've mentioned here and there, but mostly there, I'm an average guy with an unusual talent. Traveling is just something I learned how to do. I doubt that I have any particular extra this or that, but mostly that, allowing me to travel more than you.

You're talented too. I'm going to guess that you can catch twenty quarters in mid-drop off your elbow. No wait, that's me again. It's the stupidest talent you've ever seen but I can do it. And I can watch a new television series from last episode to first, or in any order if need be, and yet still follow the plot line. That's as worthless a talent as can be. It's as worthless as traveling out of my body. That's a ridiculous talent that you shouldn't be wasting your time on. Or is it? I'm surprised it took you this long to get here. I would have skipped to the end of this verbose paragraph ages ago.

As an average you, you can choose what talents you want to have. Practice makes experts. It's an expression of who you are. If you've chosen traveling as a talent to pursue it shows you are a free-minded and open soul wanting to explore and learn. Or you have some time to waste and figured what the heck. Either way, your best approach to traveling is to try some of this and some of that, but mostly some of that. You want to choose the positive things that work and toss out the things that don't work.

By observing you, the only one that matters, you can learn from your travel attempts to modify your method, adjust your sleeping schedule, fiddle with your travel plan, scrunch the pillows that prop you up, or find a soothing sound to lull you down. You can fine-tune your traveling attempts to maximize your success.

Even when you're not one hundred percent successful, all travel attempts are useful to you. You'll soon have yet another completely pointless talent to tell your family and friends all about. Well, not completely pointless. There is the thrill factor. I'll tell you about that now if you have more time to waste.

The whole point of traveling and trying to travel is the thrill. Every aspect of traveling, from your nonphysical lift-out to the return to your physical, is thrilling. Do you want to float to your comfortable chair? You can do that. That's thrilling. Do you want to hang out at the ocean but you live in the city? You can do that. That's thrilling. Do you want to visit with a loved one that you haven't seen in an age? You can do that. That's thrilling. Do you want to visit a nearby planet? You can do that. That's thrilling. Do you want to find a new perspective on reality? Well, you can do that too. At its basic level traveling comes down to your individual thrill of challenge and discovery. Traveling is a constant thrill!

PIECING THE PUZZLES

In my early years of being nonphysical my success with consciously-induced traveling was sporadic. I was averaging one "I meant to do that" travel to three "oops, I'm out again" travels. Although the unintended travels were welcome, my goal was to gain some control of the event. I eventually learned that a nonphysical travel is not just one puzzle with pieces that fit each time to cause the event. Instead, each travel is its own puzzle, which uses the same pieces as all the other puzzles, but not all the pieces are needed at any one time.

For instance: one puzzle piece in tonight's traveling puzzle is your chosen relaxation method. Did the method match the kind of day you had or how you were feeling? Was it a good method based on how much sleep you had before trying it? Did the relaxation method match your travel plan?

Your travel plan is another puzzle piece for your puzzle. Did your plan have a clear action or destination? Did you fine-tune your plan based on your experiences from previous plans?

Other puzzle pieces may be as minor as staying warm on a cold night or cool on a hot night. You take note of what specific pieces are needed for each particular attempt at traveling to better your chances for getting out. That is a completed puzzle.

A traveling puzzle constantly changes because there are 'variables' that make your attempt to travel more difficult. As I just mentioned, one variable might be that you're too cold or hot under the covers, that is corrected by the puzzle piece of either dressing for bed differently or adding/removing some of the bed linen.

A variable might be a distracting noise that you correct by the puzzle piece of using earplugs or a headset with music you like. A variable might be that you're too jumpy to relax and is corrected by the puzzle piece of doing some exercise. Your puzzle pieces are anything that counteract the variables you are experiencing at the time.

It will help with your travels to make a list of your variables as you encounter them. By recognizing the variables you learn to adjust quickly with your puzzle pieces and increase your chances at nonphysical success.

The following is a diary entry in which the variable was only a poorly constructed bed and the puzzle piece was a comfortable change of position. I chose this entry to illustrate how minor a variable can be and yet still hinder your traveling attempt. It also shows how easily a traveling puzzle can be completed using a specific puzzle piece for that moment. I didn't write my diaries to be read by you, so it's incredibly boring. But I'll provide a joke afterwards to make up for it.

November 9, 1980
After waking at about 8:30am I tried to stay relaxed and focus on traveling. Vibration was just starting when I felt some lower back pain and the vibe faded. So next I tried my right side which eased my discomfort. After about fifteen minutes I began to feel somewhat disoriented. I roused myself slightly to

discover that I was over the side of the bed and looking at the floor. Thinking nothing of this I tried to sit up and back onto the bed. It was then that I felt vibration again and realized I was out of sync. It was actually my nonphysical that was over the bed and now sitting up and away from my physical. I looked me over and saw both bodies quite clearly. I could tell the event was close to ending. I was soon back in my physical on my right side.

A chicken steps on stage and struts to the microphone to tell a joke. "Cluck cluckkkk cluck cluck?" The chicken pauses for effect. "Cluck cluck cluckkkkk cluckkkk cluck cluckkkkk!"

I didn't say I'd provide a *good* joke. You try finding a funny chicken. There are very few good chicken comedians. And none of them agreed to do my book. I had to settle for an old vaudeville chicken.

GRID LOCK

Although you may have all of your travel bases covered during an attempt, you might not be able to get beyond a certain point that I call the 'insomnia effect'. You may just hang there, stuck in your physical. You're not sleeping, nor are you fully awake, as you wait for the moment you blast from your body into the nonphysical environment. But you know what? You're trying too hard. Your control over sleep is so complete that you defeat the point you've reached and thus repeat a wall you can't beat. In other words, because rhyming is just plain silly, although you are close to the awake/asleep line you do not let yourself go. Your focus to remain alert is so intense you simply lay there on the insomniac edge. So I suggest that you try a reverse.

The following method starts as a tease that allows your physical to shut down, and ends with a subconscious pull-back of your conscious control, that is then redirected towards your travel. The tease is: "I'm going to sleep, I'm not going to sleep".

To begin the tease use a relaxation method as you normally would and have a traveling plan of destination or action. A destination would be to a specific person, place, or object. An action would be a specific task or activity to accomplish while nonphysical.

As you near the awake/asleep line ponder this thought or similar: "I am going to sleep now. I am going to give up my control and slide down to sleep. I feel myself drifting to sleep." Let yourself go. It's so easy to slip that line and cross to sleep. It's wonderful to sleep. You want to go to sleep. There you go, over the line.

Because you consciously tell yourself it's okay to sleep you are able to cross the line. There's no need for insomnia because you've told yourself that you're giving up on traveling for the night. But what your consciousness doesn't know is that subconsciously you're still desiring to travel. You've only given up control for the moment. This tiny tidbit of trickery is kept just below the surface. You know you want to travel but you're not directly thinking of it now. It's a hidden agenda at the edge of your thoughts that brings you back over the line without your conscious direction to do so. You ignore your desire to travel until it's needed so that you step over to sleep, and then you pull back to the awake/asleep line. With your physical now actually asleep, rather than just laying there, your traveling plan is all you need to get nonphysical. Your success at pulling back from the tease will increase each time you use it, thus curbing the insomnia effect and greatly increasing your chances for a travel.

PEP TALK

I believe that if you desire to travel from your body, and you know a few basic tricks, you will succeed. But desire is difficult to maintain when your travel results are slim. It's rare to have a fully conscious and controlled travel the very first time you try. It is far more likely that you will obtain mild successes over a number of attempts. It's therefore important to understand that these successes are also beneficial to your goal. Don't allow yourself to be dismayed by a few tries. Traveling may be elusive until you get the hang of assembling your puzzle pieces. To leave your body you are overcoming your previous expectations of a normal night's sleep, your old subconscious programming, and countless variables that get in your way. You will get past these obstacles with perseverance and a positive attitude. Eventually your normal night's sleep will take on a new meaning, your subconscious will respect your updated agenda, and the variables will become fewer. Try to stay focused on improving with each effort and you will. Every attempt is a success and the payoff is well worth the effort.

THE LINE

Let's review, shall we? Well, we're going to anyway, whether you want to or not. Desire is the main catalyst to getting out of your body. Relaxation and visualization methods can relax your physical body to slumber city without sending you along with it. You left your ink pen in your jacket and ruined the laundry.

On a normal night, without the intention of traveling, you lay in your bed and make the decision to relax beyond relaxation and cross the line from awake to asleep. Once you cross the line you dream a jolly mix of subconsciously pent-up thoughts and desires stirred with tidbits from your daily life. From here a few things may happen:

➢ You may dream in your physical body or dream while in your nonphysical body.

➢ You may 'wake up' while dreaming in your physical body, while it still sleeps, and 'lift-out' for a travel plan in your nonphysical body.

➤ You may 'wake up' while nonphysically 'acting out' your dream, and then re-direct your non-physical body into your travel plan.

➤ You may not wake up at all, while your bodies just sleep and dream all night.

"Cockadoodledoo," crows the old vaudeville chicken! It's morning now and time to wake up. You make a decision to cross back over the line, suppressing the urge to sleep, and off you go to start your day. As you drive to work you notice a strange blue light moving slowly across the sky and suddenly it's night time again and you're back in bed. Time just flew by didn't it? The clock reads that you've already had five hours of sleep. You've slept enough and you feel alert from the downtime you've had, and the new alien microchip in your head, but it's too early to get up and start your day again. It is then that you realize that the awake/asleep line isn't as tempting to leap across when you've already had some sleep. If you were careful you could step very slowly towards the awake/asleep line and stand on it. Your decision made, you move towards the line. You notice the slide as your physical senses shut down one by one. Typically, but not always, in this order: your physical senses of touch, sight, hearing and smell. Taste doesn't really shut down or do anything different because it's lazy. You slowly move towards the line, getting accustomed to maintaining your control. You pull back to the awake side of the line if you feel yourself sliding too quickly. You may also momentarily fall over into the asleep side of the line and then become alert and pull yourself back. Your ability to pull back from sleep indicates your increasing control near the line. It's a battle of your conscious and subconscious desire against your unconscious will.

On the awake side of the line your physical is awake and so are you. On the asleep side of the line you are dragged down to sleep as your physical goes to sleep. But when you stay on the line, between both sides, you are alert and aware while your physical body sleeps. Standing on the awake/asleep line doesn't usually happen right away. But the more you control your descent to sleep the easier it becomes to do it again. If you take one step now and two steps the next time you're getting there. And once you've reached the line it's time to go traveling.

Step Three: Visualization - Destination

Directions

Hi there you, standing near the awake/asleep line. Why are you tapping your foot in impatience? Oh, so that I'll quickly tell you what happens next. Cool your jets, I'm typing as fast as I can.

There are three different directions that you might take while near or on the awake/asleep line.

You might have a ...

1. Generalized or Specific Dream In Your Physical:

'Generalized' involves a basic idea for your dream that allows the dream to proceed as it will with limited instructions. Dreams of this type are usually unintentional, occurring on their own, but may also be intentional as I'll explain.

'Specific' involves more defined elements for your dream and your dream follows your lead. You may continually mold this type of dream while you're dreaming it. Dreams of this type are intentional.

You might also have a ...

2. Dream-Travel Outside Your Physical:

Your nonphysical travels from your physical in a dream-state either generally or specifically instructed by you. You may 'awaken' at any point while out. Dreams of this type are excellent jumping off points for traveling.

Lastly, and best, you might have a...

3. Travel Outside Your Physical:

From the awake/asleep line you bypass any dreaming at all and 'lift-out' from your physical fully alert and in control.

Dreamily

As you've read already, unless you're skipping around the book and happened upon this sentence purely by accident, visualization is a good relaxation method. It also allows you to direct your dreams. These dreams that you direct may help you to resolve a problem in your life, or may release happy memories long forgotten, or may bring you to wondrous places only you can imagine. Dreams that you direct may also launch you from your physical body.

Directing your dreams requires nothing more than visualization near the awake/asleep line.

Normally, if you were to fall over the line into sleep you'd dream anyway after a bit of time. As I mentioned, your uncontrolled dreams are usually formed of your last thoughts before succumbing to sleep and a hodgepodge of nicknacks from your subconscious. But your alert and aware presence near the awake/asleep line is the magic that deepens your visualization into a dream of your choosing. You may either allow the visualization you've created to run free, as with a generalized dream, or improvise your visualization, as with a specific dream.

You have a choice of being in the dream as yourself or someone else. You can be anything that you want. You might not be in the dream at all but simply observe a dream you've created. Your options are unlimited.

A generalized dream is a simple concept: you create a basic dream idea and let it run free. For instance, if you place yourself in a dream at a picnic on a sunny day, that's enough. The dream can now continue without your bizzybodyness interrupting every two minutes. Maybe the grill is ready for cooking. Maybe the kites are flying. Maybe birds are chirping and squirrels are running and in the nearby lake an ant rows by on a bag of sandwiches. All of these wonderful things may unfold without your direct instructions. Of course all of these wonderful things are coming from your wonderful subconscious thoughts to make them wonderful. But you are not consciously directing these small parts of your wonderful play. To you, being there at the picnic is a wonderful *ad lib* of scenery and adventure—aside from your incessant use of the word "wonderful".

Now, let's jump to a specific dream after you get me a potato off the grill at your picnic. They're done now. Bring the butter too. To continue, while I wait for my potato, if you were to visualize 'points of location and action' at your picnic you'd see that trampoline over there by the big cliff. That sure is a strange place to put a trampoline but, heck, it looks like fun. You'd visualize yourself strolling towards the trampoline and arriving there. You'd visualize climbing up onto the big round rubber surface. You'd visualize yourself taking a few trial hops. Hop hop hop hop. The rubber yields and springs back. Hop hop. You hop a little higher now, enjoying the brief freedom from gravity. You take a huge HOP. The rubber springs back launching you fifty feet into the air. It is then that you remember the trampoline is near the edge of a big cliff... So where's my potato?

While it's too late to save yourself from going over the cliff, a strong breeze catches you in mid-bounce and propels you even higher. It's probably all those toasted marshmallows you ate at the picnic making you lighter than air. The breeze carries you up and up into the clouds where you are picked up by another cross wind and a surprised flock of geese. You float out over the mountains. The air is cool and clear. The moon is just starting to rise. You continue to direct the visualization of your dream to take you where you want to go and do what you want to do.

From that specific dream, that you have while still in your physical body, let's now jump to your nonphysical 'acting out' your dream either semi-consciously or unconsciously. As I mentioned previously, your nonphysical may travel from your physical in a dream-state. It's very close to a fully-realized travel, but your consciousness is just a step over the asleep side of the line. The dream is real and vivid and you are traveling in a manner that mimics being in control, *but* you don't wake up. Your nonphysical zooms about pretending to do what you wanted to do in your dream. In one embarrassing moment your nonphysical dreamily leaps off the diving board of the neighbor's empty pool because you think it's a trampoline.

Since this is a dream-travel you may later compare what things actually are to what you thought they were when you were dreaming. In other words (because these words were just sitting around) you dreamed of a trampoline near the edge of a cliff but you remember your neighbor's diving board. Could this be a clue that you were actually traveling out of your body? Could this mean that all you have to do now is 'wake up' while you're still nonphysical? Could you use the neighbor's pool as a trigger to awaken you when you're at the pool again? Could you stop asking so many questions? Yes, yes, yes, and yes.

You can awaken, and be alert and aware at any point during a dream-travel. You may then re-direct yourself into a traveling plan and off you go. While I munch on this dream potato, that actually turned out to be your neighbor's dog's chewy toy, let me give you some ideas for recognizing that you're dreaming either in or out of your physical body.

Here's an idea. Are you dreaming right now? Maybe you are and you don't know it. I'd tell you if you're dreaming, but it's against the rules. I'm not allowed to wake you up in your dream if I'm part of your dream. Nope, this is up to you. You need to figure out if you're dreaming or not. It's not difficult. Ask yourself if you're dreaming. Now look around for clues that prove you're *not* dreaming. This small exercise in fact-checking questions your consciousness and you'll soon find yourself waking up in your dreams when the facts don't add up. As a matter of fact, if you could fact-check now we could move this whole idea along much faster.

You're sure you're awake right now. There is no doubt of it. If you fact-check now, while you're awake, the desire to look for clues will carry over into your dreams. You can't be dreaming because you arrived at work today without any effort at all. There was no alarm jarring you awake, no shower, no spilled coffee, no commute, you just *poofed* to work. You're now instantly sitting behind your desk, reading a book. Don't you think that's just a tad bit peculiar? Wellll... it's because you're dreaming! You tried to prove you're awake but the clues don't add up so you must be asleep. Now, *wake up* this very instant. You can do it. Question your waking hours and you'll question your dream hours too.

Hey, look over here. It's another idea. Remember how you discovered that the trampoline near the cliff was really your neighbor's diving board over an empty pool? You were thinking that you must have had a dream-travel and you were right. Because you are so fond of trampolines this is bound to happen again. You'll find yourself back at your neighbor's pool bouncing on the board. Been here before... Something going on... Been here before... Something going on... Hey wait, you've been here *before*, haven't you? You were on that diving board just the other day when you dreamed you bounced over the cliff. That would seem to indicate that you're dreaming again. And that's the perfect time to *wake up!* If you're at the same place or action as you were before, either in or out of your body, you must be dreaming.

This idea is too obvious. You are sitting in a chair in the dark by the fish-bowl on the table. Your little fishy is in there and flipping fins at you. Flip fishy flip. The glow of fishy's water-heater clicks on and clicks off. Fishy swims over to the part of the bowl nearest you and begins to say something with bubbles. With great fishy fervor the bubbles form and float to the surface where they pop into fishy's important message: *Wake Up!* How many odd things have to happen in a dream before you get the message that fishy is trying to send? If it's really odd you are obviously dreaming.

With those ideas in mind let's jump one last time. Although dreams are an excellent way to focus your awareness, and introduce you to your many states of consciousness, they are not your final goal. Aside from dreaming in and out of your body, and either waking up in your dream or not, the most exciting and interesting experience occurs when you reach the awake/asleep line but *do not* slip over to the sleep side.

Being there on the line between awake and asleep you suddenly realize that you have two bodies. You have your lovely physical body sleeping soundly in the bed and, amazingly now, you have a lighter body floating there just slightly out of sync. Prove it to yourself by waving your arms around. Put your control into this lighter body and, without effort, simply wave your arms a bit to confirm that you are in a separate body from the one that sleeps. This other body is you. You can direct it where to go and what to do.

Next Stop Anywhere

Once you're on the awake/asleep line you may be pondering how to get out of your body. That's good to ponder. Move to the head of the class for being so smart. No, hang on, that's my desk. You can't sit there and get your feet off my doughnuts. *Yick*, you may as well keep them now. Take my coffee too. I'll go sit at your desk.

While there are many fun and interesting ways to leisurely get out of your physical body, we'll start first with getting you out of your physical *quickly*. You'll want to put some distance between you and your physical to avoid being pulled right back in by a random thought. I'll explain more on this 'rubber-band' effect soon but for now we'll just get you out of you and put you someplace where you won't jump right back into you.

Picking a 'destination', as part of your travel plan, is best done before reaching the awake/asleep line. You want to reach the line and then launch yourself into your travel. There is no time while teetering on the line to waffle on about where you want to go and what you want to do. For your first destination pick a place that's not too far away. Your backyard is fine or even a few miles distant. Think of a place where you like to hang out, or somewhere that holds a fond memory, or pick a destination where you may learn or achieve something by being there. Let the destination draw you to it. Put yourself there. You are already there.

You may also use a person as a destination, allowing your emotional attraction to draw you to them. You 'feel' and 'reach' for the person. You focus on their face or their laughter or something that endears them to you.

Your destination may also be an 'object of attachment' such as a cherished family portrait that sits on the mantle or that jar filled with buttons that you carry with you everywhere.

As part of your destination instruct yourself to know when you're there. *I'm aware when I'm there. I'm aware when I'm there.* This instruction will help you to remain alert and can also snap you back to awareness should you begin to dream-travel.

To combine the destination types you'd visit dear old Aunt Gladys who lives by the lake in that great log cabin where you accidentally left your jar of buttons the last time you visited.

Just like waving your nonphysical arms it's effortless to travel out of your body from the awake/asleep line. You pull your destination towards you as you are drawn towards it. Your destination literally yanks you from your body to get there.

Arriving at your destination may be instantaneous, as preferred in your early travels, or more leisurely by including specific actions in your travel plan. An example of a specific action would be taking your normal route to get to your aunt's cabin but while floating two hundred feet up to admire the view.

Less Is More And More Is More

Well, that's it. You now know everything you need to know about traveling out of your body. Yes, you have all the basics. You relax, your physical falls asleep, you reach the awake/asleep line, and off you go. Well done. I can just kick back and relax now while you go on your merry way. Bye, have a good time. No need to clutter yourself with more information on traveling when it works just fine already. Are you buying any of this? Well, for a change, I'm not joking. Traveling is not that complicated. The basics I've explained work their magic just fine without knowing all of the rest I'm about to tell you. You could stop here if you wanted and read no further. But then you'd miss the spooky story coming up in the very next chapter!

DANGER IN THE DRIVEWAY

There is nothing like traveling nonphysically. You're going to love the short trip across your bedroom. You're going to love flying straight up, blasting into the night sky like a bottle rocket. You're going to love floating around looking at this and that, mostly that. And you're really going to love being out of your body without a trouble in the world. Except for that creepy-looking thing over there by the fence. You might want to avoid that thing. That reminds me of a spooky story I mentioned in the last chapter. I guess I'll tell that story.

I really enjoy being out. I suppose that's obvious because I wrote a book about it. But I mean more specifically *how* I love it. I love the 'vibration' that I feel sometimes before I separate from my physical. I love wandering around the neighborhood. I love visiting Mars—but more on that some other time. I love everything about the experience except for that creepy-looking thing over there by the fence. That thing reminds me of a story I was going to tell you. I mentioned it in the last chapter, and then in this chapter already, and again just now. I guess I'll tell that story.

When I first started traveling I didn't know what it was. I really believed that these nonphysical excursions were just incredibly vivid dreams. Of course, some folks would say that's what traveling is, which is fine with me. But traveling was not my choice and I couldn't help falling out of my body. I would wake up, nonphysically on the floor, more times than in bed. I'd simply roll-over, as a normal sleeper would do, but I'd leave my physical behind.

In addition to waking up near my bed I'd wake up in other places. I'd wake up at the local shopping strip and the recreation center and the school playground and the creek behind my house. I'd wake up floating underwater at the community pool. Oddly enough, this didn't scare me although it was an unusual feeling. My nonphysical didn't require oxygen and, although I didn't know it then, my physical in bed was breathing just dandy while I was away. Although travels were not my choice in the beginning I could deal with them. They were weird but not usually scary. Unlike that creepy-looking thing over there by the fence. That thing reminds me of a story I was going to tell you. I mentioned it in the last chapter, and then in this chapter twice already, and again just now. That's four times I've mentioned it. So I guess I'll tell that story.

Let me just open this creaking closet door. Come on in and get comfortable on the dusty, cobwebbed pillows. I'll prop up a flashlight on this creepy-looking thing here in the corner. That reminds me of a story...

It was a bright cheery nine year-old morning and, as usual, I was out of my body. The sun was just coming up, the family still lay asleep, and my constant longing to shorten my bedtime had once again launched me somewhere. Today's somewhere turned out to be the front steps of my home. I was just floating around enjoying the freedom. I had no concept whatsoever of what I was doing but I was outside when I shouldn't have been and no one even knew I was gone. No one except for that creepy-looking thing over there by the fence at the end of the driveway. It seemed to know I wasn't where I was supposed to be. I had ignored the thing at first. It wasn't really bothering me from over there. It was just kind of hanging around in the distance while I leaped off the stairs and leaped over the hedge and leaped back up the stairs. Leaping is the greatest fun when you're nonphysical. What joy to completely ignore that creepy thing over there by the fence. What a hoot to pay absolutely no mind to that creepy thing sliding up the driveway. What a joke to totally miss the creepy thing now within an inch of my playful self. And then that son of a bungee-cord grabbed me. Its arms or whatever they were wrapped two and three times around my body and held me tight. I wasn't being strangled so much as immobilized. If I struggled one way, and made some room to free myself, the arms gripped me tighter from another direction. I tugged and pushed and pulled against its stretchy appendages. And still this whatever it was just hung in there. The clingy parasite had soon exhausted my ability to cope and my fear began to rise. My wits gone, and losing the battle, I did what any other nine year-old might do in my situation. I began to cry. I had no idea what I was doing or what the thing was doing and I couldn't get away from it and the fight was just too much. "Wahhhh," I wept nonphysically. The crying had no effect at all on the thing. Aside from hanging on to me it didn't seem to care what I did. So I screamed. I wailed for my mother as strong as I ever had. Although the scream was nonphysical it produced an effect. I was immediately snapped back to my physical in bed, leaving that ridiculous thing out on the front steps. Sure, it was the easy way out but that's what kids do. They call for help. I had no way of knowing at the time that the act of calling out for help actually triggers an instant return to your physical. It's a last-ditch effort that works every time. You can't get lost or trapped outside your body. It's self-preservation—if you can't fight you take flight. Calling for my mom was my emotional reaction to save myself. It's a safe-guard of the 'rubber-band' effect that I mentioned earlier and will again.

Unfortunately, my fun for the morning was not over. Following my return to bed I mellowed out for a few minutes and rationalized that the travel was still nothing more than a "real-dream", unlikely to occur twice. But I was wrong three times. The second time was about ten minutes after that first return. I started to drift back towards the awake/asleep line and zipped out to the driveway. In less than five seconds guess who came creeping in my direction? It came within inches of me before I screamed back to my physical. I had enough of this game and got out of bed for the day. But, on the following morning, without a conscious choice to go playing in the "dream", I found myself out on the front steps again. The mindless vine was right there too. You know where this is going so I won't say it again. I made it back to my bedroom in the usual fashion. And that was my last out of body travel for about a year.

As an adult I can analyze the annoying clinging thing I encountered as just being annoyingly clingy. But as a child I was terrified. I didn't seem to have any control over the "real-dreams" which meant I would never be safe from attack. As it turns out, the clinging thing taught me something. I learned that I actually did have the ability to stay put in my physical body. My anxiety of the thing was so overwhelming that I turned off the non-physical travels completely. For almost a year I didn't think about "real-dreaming". I pushed my bed close to the wall and wrapped up tight at night. I had a mind-set to stay put and stay safe. It worked.

As I've explained, an unexperienced traveler doesn't need to understand how the nonphysical works to do it. My youthful desire would send me traveling but I was unfamiliar with the nonphysical environment. I was the perfect bait for that clinging thing. It took me the span of a year to "grow up" beyond its grasp.

When I was ten I ventured back to the "real-dream" that I now know as traveling. The thing was no where to be found. I haven't seen it since those bright cheery mornings in the driveway. I have seen other creepy things, though. I don't let them get close to me.

While you're nonphysical there are others that you might run into. If you're out and your neighbor is out and you're both on a similar travel you might meet. Or you might run into my pal, Huggy

Stuff. I thought a cute name would make it less scary. Intruding entities are out there, but rarely where you are. Don't worry yourself. They are more apt to prey on the unaware which you are not any longer. You also know now that if a thing were to approach, bother, or attack you, it's a simple matter to will yourself back to your physical in bed. And, if you don't want to go back to bed, Huggy Stuff and his ilk can be kept at a distance by thinking 'stay away thoughts'. You simply put up a wall blocking the intrusion.

It was a big deal to me as a child but nonphysical encounters are usually innocent and always interesting. You can 'feel' for others you meet to sense if they are good or not good. If they're not good, and you get into trouble, getting back to your physical is virtually foolproof, which is perfect for you. *Zing.* You won't be forever trapped out of body by someone you meet or someplace you go. Always remember that you can rise above your less than pleasant travels and that Huggy Stuff is just a cuddly muffin.

Step Four: Direct Lift-Out

Three, Two, One: Lift-Out

Following your success at getting quickly out of your body, in as graceless a manner as possible, your goal is to consciously control a start to finish travel by a 'direct lift-out'. A 'lift-out' is any method utilized by the nonphysical body to separate from the physical. A 'direct lift-out' is a method that you would consciously choose and control to separate from the physical.

A direct lift-out has many benefits over an uncontrolled lift-out. For starters, you consciously experience the separation of your nonphysical from your physical. It's an incredible feeling. One moment you're in bed and the next you're sliding out from your own body. It's a triumph of your efforts that immediately changes your purely physical perspective on life. A direct lift-out allows you to be more adaptive with your actions as you move towards your destination, rather than being instantly away and instantly back. A direct lift-out also helps you to maintain a more continuous level of conscious control and recall more details of your travel when you 'return' to your physical. Lastly, a direct lift-out propels you faster from the precarious awake/asleep line. The direct lift-out becomes the first 'action' of your travel plan. You hit the line and instruct yourself to roll out from your body. Or you hit the line and sit up from your body. Or you hit the line and float to the ceiling. Or you hit the line and stand up and walk away. Simple actions, that you instruct yourself to do, occur because you're on the line while your physical is sleeping and your nonphysical is willing. To further plan your direct lift-out action, you can give yourself a trial run by physically doing what you will do when you hit the line. Except for that lift-out where you float to the ceiling. I tried that once with balloons and didn't come down for a week.

SIGNAL RECEIVED

Well, hi there. I see you on the awake/asleep line. You don't know you're there yet but you are. You're lazily drifting. Your physical body has been asleep five minutes now. You might slip over to the sleep side if that alarm doesn't go off soon. Tick tick tick. *Zapppp!* A 'vibration' sweeps over your body. It's not painful but it's powerful. Your physical body is immediately catatonic. It would take an extreme force of will to even move a finger. The vibration continues to course through your body. You can smooth out the vibration by mentally pushing it down your body and then up your body and then down your body and then up your body, creating a smoother wave. Or you could just stop all your hem hawing and fly out of your bed.

Vibration is just one of many 'signals' you may be treated to during your attempts to travel non-physically. 'Signals' are a flare going up up up and lighting the sky. They are your get-out-of-your-body alarm clock. Unless a lift-out occurs very quickly, following your arrival on the line, you will likely enjoy at least one signal and possibly a combination of signals.

Feel The Vibe

Vibration is the most interesting of the signals and the most unsettling. It feels electric but it's not. It seems like it should hurt but it doesn't. It completely shuts you off from your physical senses but it turns on your nonphysical senses. Vibration is a signal that you are on the awake/asleep line and is felt only while your physical and nonphysical are in close proximity to each other. Your perception of the two vibrational frequencies of physical and nonphysical, as they overlap, creates the effect. Your physical is unresponsive because your consciousness is now nonphysical. If you really wanted to, you could force your physical to move. This transfers your conscious control back, away from your nonphysical. Your nonphysical then re-syncs with your physical and your fun is done. That rhymes. A better option is to recognize that vibration is a signal that you're on the awake/asleep line and you're ready for lift-out. If you're feeling vibe, it's time to fly. That mostly rhymes.

If you were to do nothing during vibration, just allowing it to zap over you, the signal could last many minutes. Although it frightened me as a child it's not without its charm. You might enjoy letting it run its course or try smoothing it out for practice.

Vibration is always present as part of the lift-out process but may go unnoticed if the jump from physical to nonphysical happens quickly or if the lift-out happens while you're in a semiconscious or unconscious state.

Of more interest, regarding vibration, your physical vibrates at the same frequency—let's call it 'speed'—as other things in the physical environment. Your nonphysical vibrates at a variable speed, tuned to the nonphysical environments that you visit.

Your faster vibrating nonphysical body can walk through walls just because it's fun to do. You'll feel each layer of the wall if you pass through slowly enough. Look for that money dear old Aunt Gladys is hiding behind the medicine cabinet.

On the rare occasion that your nonphysical is vibrating very closely to that of the physical environment you may bump into physical objects and feel they can't be passed through. This is easily overcome by a strong desire to get past the physical object. This focus increases the speed at which you vibrate so that the object is no longer 'solid' to you. Like so. You are out of your body. You wander down the hall. You turn the corner. You run into your front door. It feels solid. You desire to pass through the door. You *want* to get through the door! Your demand triggers an increase in your vibrational speed beyond the slower vibrating physical object. You slide easily through the door.

SURGING ONWARD

What a rush that last chapter was, huh? That chapter got me all flushed with excitement. Wooo, my face feels red. You know how you feel on a roller coaster or when you see someone you really like or when you watch a scary movie and it surprises you or when you read a chapter really really fast trying to get to the point that the idiot author is trying to make? What a rush, huh? That's what the 'surge' signal feels like too.

Surge feels like nonphysical adrenaline. You'll be comfortable in your bed, right near the awake/asleep line, and the surge signal will sweep over you in an instant like a blast of heat over the desert. You can maintain this heightened rush for many minutes while remaining in near-sync with your physical body. Your control is now in your nonphysical but can be transferred back to your physical by force of your desire to do so. But rather than doing that you can use the surge signal as an indication that it's okay to go flying now.

ROLL OVER YOU'RE SNORING

My goodness you're a loud snorer. I could hear you snoring from way down in the cellar where I was looking for a bottle of something that goes with tofu. Apparently nothing does. Your snoring is making the light fixtures rattle. Pots and pans are falling out of the cabinets. Your neighbors called to ask if you're feeling the earthquake too. You have to be the loudest snorer I have ever heard in all my live-long days.

I now take all of that back about your snoring. You snore a bit but it's not so bad hearing you snore from here in the other room. It's comforting to hear you breathing deeply in the distance, getting all of that good rest that your physical body needs. But your snoring sure sounds loud to you since you're the one doing it. It's like eating potato chips in a quiet theater. *CRUNCH CRUNCH SNORE SNORE.* You can hear yourself snoring louder than any other sound entering your ears. Your snore drowns out everything with its bombastic thunder! Hey, wait a minute. You're *snoring*. You're laying there in bed and you are snoring. That must mean that your physical body is sleeping. And that must mean that your nonphysical is just hanging around waiting to go somewhere. And all that combined must mean that snoring is a signal that you can't ignore even if you wanted to.

CHILL OUT

Is that all you're wearing to bed? I hope you have a nice warm blanket because that birthday suit isn't going to keep you toasty when your temperature drops on the awake/asleep line. It isn't much of a temperature change, maybe a tenth of a degree, but it sure feels cold when you're on the line. It's a good signal if you're warm enough in bed to notice it without being distracted by it.

To recall something earlier that I typed, and you may or not have read, the temperature drop signal is helpful but creates a variable in your traveling puzzle. The variable is you perceiving your body as cold when you reach the awake/asleep line. This slight discomfort distracts you from your attempt to travel. So you fit the puzzle piece that corrects the variable and you go romping out of your body. The puzzle piece here is preparing to be warm. While you don't want to smother yourself in heavy blankets or restrictive clothing, you do want to find a happy compromise so that your physical is warm enough when the temperature drop signal tells you it's time to go traveling.

SEEING WITH YOUR EYES CLOSED

To quote me from earlier, which just seems wrong, "I was over the side of the bed and looking at the floor... It was actually my nonphysical that was over the bed... I looked me over and saw both bodies quite clearly."

I should write the rest of the book like that, with dots and then right to the next thought. Saves a lot time don't you think... The end.

While you lay there, which you do a lot of with this nonphysical hobby, you may discover that you're looking at your room. This wouldn't be unusual except that your eyes are closed. You see your ceiling and there's your dresser and over there is your fishbowl on the table. You see all of this while your head is on the pillow and your eyes are closed. If you wanted to you could move your field of vision by thinking to do so. You could look behind you if you felt so inclined while reclined.

You're now 'seeing' nonphysically. You are slightly above and out of sync with your closed physical eyes. It may take a moment to realize. It's subtle at first. It's almost as if you forgot your eyeglasses and everything is fuzzy. But then you start to recognize shapes in your room and, as you think about seeing, it becomes clearer. Seeing nonphysically is a sense that takes very little practice to master. As you progress you'll find that you can also 'see' down to tiny details and 'see' great distances.

Seeing with your eyes closed is a signal that your nonphysical is ready to go go go. So see the window, go out the window.

Pseudo Sounds And Sights

Ring ring ring. Hey you! The cat just ran by. Trumpet blast. Wind howls. *Vroooom.* The television is too loud. Rooster crows. Aunt Gladys slams the medicine cabinet. None of this is happening.

As you reach the awake/asleep line you may encounter a wide assortment of playful skits, kicked up from your subconscious, that distract you from your travel plan. They are all fake. Some of the pseudo sounds and sights can be entertaining and some annoying.

It's unlikely the phone is going to ring at exactly the same time as you reach the awake/asleep line. The cat is outside. No one is playing the trumpet. The winds are calm. There's no loud car driving by or television blaring or rooster crowing. Aunt Gladys is sleeping, not hiding money behind the— I mean slamming the medicine cabinet. Nothing at all has changed in your quiet room in your comfortable bed where your physical body sleeps.

This fakery is a signal that you're ready to lift-out. Your nonphysical is still in near-sync with your physical that is trying to sleep and dream. You don't have to go along for that ride. Once you separate from your physical the pseudo sounds and sights will stop. This confirms they are fake.

The other way to confirm a fake may also end your attempt to travel for the evening. If it's a pseudo sound that you question, focus on hearing that sound though your ears. This triggers your physical sense of hearing, like straining to hear a faint sound in the distance. Unfortunately, it also puts your conscious control ever so slightly back in your physical. If you rouse your physical too much the show is over. So once you've confirmed the pseudo sound is fake you want to back off from your physical and return to your deeper level at the awake/asleep line.

The same type of test is used to confirm a pseudo sight but it's more precarious. You want to open one eye just a fraction to confirm the pseudo sight is fake. The physical act of opening your eye places your full conscious control back into your physical. Unlike your sense of hearing, you must make muscles move to see physically. For that to happen you have to be back in your body. You may be able to confirm the fake and then back off from your physical, allowing your consciousness to return to the near-sync of the nonphysical. But sometimes once the sleeping giant is awakened it's up for good.

Pseudo sounds and sights are a signal that you're on the line. You can practice with them, moving your control from nonphysical to physical, and then back again. Or you can notice them, then ignore them, and move on to your travel plan.

Lastly, if you keep hearing the phone, each time you reach the awake/asleep line, you could just unplug it before going to bed. Same goes for Aunt Gladys.

Connect The Dots

When I was eleven years old I began to notice a phenomenon that I now call 'dots'. Dots are a rolling mass of tiny pinpoints that you 'see' behind your closed eyelids just prior to a nonphysical travel. You may also 'see' the dots with your eyes open in a very dark room but this places emphasis on your physical body during a time when you're striving to let that body sleep. Dots cling together by the thousands in one mass as they move. As your travel conditions become optimum the size of the mass increases. Although the size of the mass will vary the dots always remain the same size. I know this isn't particularly exciting information but it is useful.

You may have already noticed the friendly dots in your nonphysical attempts. They are not something you create by desire but if you look for them prior to a travel they'll be there. You can use the floating mass of dots as both a signal that you're close to traveling and as a focus to help get you there. Gently 'push' the dots in a direction you choose. Try to move them in a smooth arc rather than jumping them from one spot to another. Immerse yourself in the movement of the dots, guiding them where you want them to be. After a short time you'll notice that the dots' intensity, and your ability to see them, has increased. Also by this time your physical has likely fallen asleep while you remained alert on the awake/asleep line. You may begin to notice other signals as a clue to being ready for a travel. So bid the helpful dots adieu and lift-out from your body, you.

You Tease

To further explain how easy it is to lift-out from the awake/asleep line you'll play a game. The game is called 'Here I Go'. You play it by getting into your bed and then telling yourself to do something that you have no intention of doing. "I'm going to roll over on my side in a moment, here I go." And then you don't do anything. Pretty simple game, huh? "I really want to roll over now. I'm going to roll over on my side any second now. Here I go." Now *don't* do it. Tell yourself that you are going to perform an action that forces you to move your physical body, but then just lay there.

Now we'll move this game to the awake/asleep line where, just like a dream-travel, your imminent movement that never physically occurs forces your nonphysical into action. When you're on or near the awake/asleep line you intentionally choose an action that requires movement but you refuse to let your physical be the body to do it. "I'm going to stand up now and stroll over to the table. Here I go."

It's like scratching an itch. There's the itch and your thought process that precedes your actual movement to scratch it. Even though you haven't made a move to do so yet the trigger to scratch has already occurred. A stress of desire builds until you allow yourself to scratch or you scratch without even recognizing that you're doing so. The same goes for a nonphysical lift-out. From the line, your desired action triggers either a conscious direct lift-out and travel, or a subconscious indirect lift-out and dream-travel. One way or the other you're strolling to the table.

A lift-out from your physical is just a simple gesture of instructions. Because your physical sleeps while you remain alert, your nonphysical listens and obeys most of the time. The nonphysical can also be obstinate, but more on that later.

You'll soon find that a direct lift-out requires only a whim of decision without all the teasing. Your intention to move nonphysically is recognized and imprinted on your subconscious. You learn to jump from the awake/asleep line to a direct lift-out on command. This became apparent to me years ago when I went to grab the newspaper at my front door. I tried to pick up the paper three times before I realized that my physical was still back in bed. The first thing I did when I returned to my bed was laugh out loud. Which brings me to the following ridiculous notion.

Check Please

Let's say you don't believe any of this hoohah about traveling out of your body. Go ahead, you can say it. You won't hurt my feelings. It's fine that you remain in your bed all night. It also saves me from telling you a safety tip for traveling and that gives me ten minutes for a cup of espresso. You're the best.

Now let's say you do believe in the hoohah of traveling out of your body. It's your hope to go nonphysically here and there, mostly there, enjoying the freedom of your newly found hobby. That takes back my ten minutes and my cup of espresso, giving me time to tell you a safety tip for traveling. You're still the best.

It's nighttime for you now and you're standing by the window, overlooking the garden which is about thirty feet below. You've been telling yourself to get out of your body when you reach the awake/asleep line and here you are at the window preparing to jump out onto the flowers. The tapestry of petals beckons you forward and you leap. *Wait.* Hang on there, you. Before you go headlong make sure you're actually out of your body and not moving physically.

Similar to unconsciously sleep-walking you may semi-consciously control the movement of your physical but you're not aware of doing so. It's like when you're near to dreaming and you imagine that you're catching or throwing a ball. Suddenly your arm flies up. You may be alert and everything seems nonphysical but check it out to be safe. This is especially true when you are close to your physical body in a normal setting such as your home. It would be most upsetting to read of your physical plunge from the window in the tabloids: *DECEASED BRINGS OWN FLOWERS.*

In your early traveling, if at any time there is a question of physical danger you should perform a few simple tests to verify that you are indeed nonphysical. When you find yourself at the window, and you will, because they are just so darn fun to fly through, stay right where you are and hop up and down a bit. If you're nonphysical your hops will be a hop up and then a float down. Hop up, float down. It's nothing at all like hopping physically. If you're still not sure, look at the floor. You may be 'standing' on it, feeling its very slight resistance, or floating just above it. If you're floating you're out. But if you're 'standing' on it, making it difficult to determine if you're semi sleep-walking, you need to test further that you're nonphysical. Gently poke your hand at a wall. If you poke into a solid barrier, that remains despite your best effort, you're physical. If you feel a slight resistance, and then your hand goes through, you're out of body. Feel free to fling to the flowers.

In addition to windows you should check that you're really out of body before leaping off furniture and jumping from balconies. You'll find that testing your surroundings also heightens your 'awareness' while nonphysical which, not coincidentally, is the topic we are about to visit.

STEP FIVE: AWARENESS

EXPLORER

HOOOOOOOOGAH! the ship's horn bellows. It sure is foggy out here. We can't see a thing and I sure hope that's your hand on my shoulder. Everything is so muted and melty. There's the shoreline but we can't see any of the buildings. What we need is a really good pair of binoculars like that pair that just appeared next to the orange toilet ring. Flotation device, whatever. Let's just have a look-see now and... dagnabit, we are back at your neighbor's pool again. It's filled with water now, at least. And his dog is woofing at us. That explains the ship horn. Good thing we had the binoculars so we could focus on the details of our surroundings, which heightened our awareness. We should try to remember to do this next time we're out of body. Since our nonphysical 'awareness' can sometimes be blurry, and we want it sharp, it's important to quiz ourselves with 'details' of where we are and what we're doing. Don't you agree? Nod yes.

You don't actually need nonphysical binoculars to see where you are and what you're up to. You only need to look around and notice things. 'Detailing' throughout your travel provides the spark that keeps you aware. You focus on the smaller questions to bring clarity to the larger event. This provides the benefits of improved control during your travel and a clearer memory imprint after returning to your physical. It also makes re-visiting your destination easier the next time because you can recall specifics that allow you to 'think yourself there'. Why you'd want to go back to your neighbor's pool though is beyond me.

There you are traveling. Are you flying, running, jumping, sliding, swimming? How do you look nonphysically? Are you are normal, wispy, transparent, undefined? What time of day is it? Do you see road signs? Do you see people? What are they doing? How's the weather? Cloudy, sunny, snowy? Do you recognize where you are or is it someplace new? Does it seem like the physical environment you know or is it something different? Is the fence leaning, is the grass too tall, is that a frog? Look at things. That's the whole joy of being out. Become aware of the entire experience by paying close attention.

In addition to seeing details of your nonphysical travels you may also 'feel' the details of your surroundings. You can 'touch' an icy-cold lamppost without the fear of sticking to it or the pain of frostbite. You can 'touch' lava without the obvious side-effects. You can touch the grass and flowers in your garden. And here's something more amazing.

Float down into the grass and enjoy the freshness. Yes, you can 'smell' while nonphysical by desiring to do so. It's not like your physical sense of smell. The aroma merges with your nonphysical so that you are part of it. I suggest that you start out with grass and flowers before you go investigating the trash bin at the end of the block.

When you first begin to travel nonphysically in the physical environment it's entertaining and interesting to 'tap' an obstacle before plowing on through it. Move to a wall or your desk or that stack of bricks that you have in the shed, put your nonphysical arms out in front of you, and tap tap tap. You'll feel only slight resistance as your nonphysical fingers merge and pass through the physical object. If the object has layers, like a wall, you can feel each layer as you pass through.

Moving nonphysically will often send you hurtling through things faster than you can tap them. When this occurs, relax and enjoy the ride. Tapping isn't required. Tapping and 'detailing' are tools that improve your awareness. They help you to understand being newly nonphysical.

Just like when you were a child, everything is new and must be explored before you can know it. So look at and get into everything. Anyone can just stumble through the nonphysical environment, but you will actually be part of it. Explore your new world. Be aware!

MICRO MANAGING

Hello again. I'm back from the last chapter. Did you miss me? Well, I missed you anyway. To continue with 'detailing' I'm going to show you a trick. Let me just find my notes here in the office. Well, not an office actually. It's more like a bunch of uncomfortable chairs surrounded by scraps of things I'm working on. I wonder where that scrap is? Ah, there it is on the floor in the corner next to my paperclips and pushpins. And what's That? I never noticed That before. I wonder how long That has been there? I better get a closer look at That right this second. Well look at That. It's an itsy bitsy spider. He's tiny. And look, he's waving. He's holding up a sign. It says: "Stop staring at me. Go observe in another corner". Such a surly spider. But he's right, it's important to pay attention to the small details of your surroundings. At least I think that's what he means. Maybe he's just telling me to stop hanging around. That's a spider's favorite pun.

It's our nature to selectively ignore one part of our surroundings while paying close attention to another. That's how perception works. Right now I'm blocking out the sounds of a lawn mower and some dogs barking. I'm also ignoring the little spider and his sign. These parts that surround me have been muted so that I can focus exclusively on writing this chapter. In short, way too late for that, the parts are still there but I'm not.

It's the same with you. You are presently reading this chapter and blocking out the office chatter or the dish washer or the cat meowing or a distant corner of the room. Those parts are still there but you are not. At other times, when you do think of those parts, they may receive your full attention or be toned-down or filtered. It's all up to your agenda of importance.

You utilize the exact same agenda when you leave your physical body. You might recall one small part of your travel in intricate detail while ignoring how you even got out in the first place. Sometimes your travel is crystal clear and sometimes it's foggy. Again, it's all up to your agenda of importance. You decide what you want to see and recall. Your alertness level also plays a part in your perception. You might blearily stroll through your travel and recall only a few pieces of the event or you might be full of pep and determination while observing everything. On that exciting night you could experience the whole of the travel from the awesome lift-out to the amazing return.

The trick to recalling more details, and improving your awareness, is as simple as spying a surly spider in a selected spot. As a matter of fact, not much but some, let's practice now. Pick a corner, any corner. Pick one corner and position yourself to look at it from a much different angle than you could normally view it at a glance. Get right up on that corner from the odd vantage. This is good for three reasons. One, it teaches you to detail so that you can do it while traveling. Two, it challenges your perspective. You would not normally view from this vantage while physical but you might while nonphysical. Later, you can use that different perspective to recognize a travel while it's happening. And three, it's funny to watch you get into that silly position.

To show you how serious I am about this I am going to get up from my chair now and visit a corner of this office. Well, not an office actually. You do the same. Are you ready? The aim of this exercise is to observe your corner in as much detail as possible from an odd angle. Don't hurt yourself. You're no spring chicken. That's a chicken's favorite pun. It isn't much but it makes them laugh.

I lucked out with my corner. This corner seems mostly clean here, looking at it on my right side and slightly upside down. Let's take a closer look. Yes, it looks fine except for a few cat hairs. The baseboard here is colored with an off-white paint that gives way to brown wood as it meets the carpet. The carpet kind of squooshes under the baseboard. The carpet fibers stick out in all sorts of sizes and directions. There's a phone cord, answering machine cord, table lamp cord, and some other cord that I have no idea what it does. As the cords meet over the corner they touch one particular carpet fiber that is longer than all the rest. It curves up from the carpet at a thirty degree angle. The fiber has thin vertical support-lines in it, like those found in packing tape. The top of the fiber is serrated. I am now focusing on those thin jagged edges at the top of that carpet fiber. Now I'm right there on the peak of a fiber and looking into the valley before the next peak. That's one centimeter of my home. The whole tour could take awhile.

How was your corner? Speak up, I can't hear you. In addition to observing details and odd angles, to increase your awareness while traveling, you can use your intricate detailing of your corner to send yourself there. When you're on the awake/asleep line you literally pull yourself out and to your corner by recalling the tiny details. If you were me and writing this book you'd see the baseboard as it meets the carpet. You'd see the cords and the fiber. You'd see the edges and the valleys of that fiber. Your micro-focus pulls you to that centimeter of previously ignored space. Sure, you'll be flinging yourself into a wall but it doesn't hurt at all and it's funny. So off you goo. That's a baby's favorite pun.

STEP SIX: TRAVEL

KNOW KNOWS

L a la la you sing as you nonphysically float here
and there, mostly there. It sure is good to not
know how things work nonphysically. That's just
extra mumbo jumbo la la la. So much better to just
float around. It's better here than back in bed la
la... Pow, you're back in bed.

There are some things you should know about
traveling nonphysically and I'm just the guy to tell
you those things. I'm particularly knowledgeable
about such things because I've made plenty of mis-
takes while traveling. You may now benefit from
my stupidity. I mean, *experience.*

THOUGHT EQUALS ACTION

Just as your physical body moves by conscious,
subconscious, and sometimes unconscious
thought, your nonphysical also responds to instructions from your varied states of consciousness. But there is a major difference between mov-

ing physically and moving nonphysically. When you move physically you think to go here or there or do this or that, mostly that, and then you move into action. Along the way sometimes you change your mind about what you're doing and do something else or you decide to do nothing at all. But when you're moving nonphysically the action responds instantaneously to your thought process if you're not careful. There is no delay of any kind worth mentioning so I won't mention it. Any whim at all of conscious or subconscious action may initiate an immediate response, giving you no opportunity to redirect.

It sure is marvelous to be standing by your bed. You're looking down at you sleeping there. You are so cute in your cuddly bunny pajamas. You just want to reach out and touch that little cotton tail. Pow, you're back in bed. You have got to stop paying so much attention to your physical body. The idea is to get away from it, not hang about in the bedroom admiring yourself. While you're so close, your nonphysical connection to your physical is at its super strongest. It can yank you right back into you just by you thinking about it. It would take a zillionth of a millisecond and you'd be back in that ol' potato sack. So don't think about it. Instead, move into your traveling plan. Get away from your physical using the actions you set forth for yourself. Go where you planned to go and accomplish your goals. Put some distance between you and you. This prevents being pulled back into bed before you have a chance to change your mind.

After you've been out a few times you may observe your physical or stay close by and wander around your home but you must avoid accidentally thinking yourself back into bed. Even at a great distance from your physical a random thought about your body in bed can send you hurtling back in less time than it takes to type this sentence and I'm a pretty fast typist. So what if I left out punctuation. But from a distance you have a chance at redirecting your action. The one or two seconds you may have before arriving to your bed is plenty of time to change your course.

A return to your physical is not the only result of misdirected thought. You may struggle to reach your desired destination or never reach it. You may find it difficult to control your movements as if being tossed in a strong wind.

By staying focused to your traveling plan you negate confusing and random thoughts that may pull you back or lead you astray. If your travel is a destination to a nearby park you'd lift-out and stay focused on your chosen route and the final destination of reaching the park. You may observe, as 'non-directing' thoughts, what you find while on the way to the park but keep your primary actions geared to your plan. If your thoughts wander and you find yourself misdirected, pull in the reins.

If your travel is a task, you would plan what you hope to accomplish or learn. Your goal might be to practice your nonphysical movement. You would stay focused to the planned movements, thus minimizing the chance for random thoughts. I want to fly straight up. I want to stop. I want to move to my right. I want to go faster. I want to slow down. I want I want I want.

It's good to have a basic traveling plan since you may find yourself suddenly out without having planned anything else or you may become misdirected from the plan you originally wanted to do. Your basic plan should be something that you don't mind repeating. For instance of an instance, there's a gazebo near my home. I've repeatedly instructed myself to visit the gazebo in the event that I suddenly find myself out or misdirected. I've also instructed myself to 'wake up' when I find myself at the gazebo. This preset plan places me in a familiar setting, peaks my awareness, and puts some distance between the nonphysical me and the physical me wearing koala pajamas.

Desire Equals Perception

The waiter brings you your delicious dinner. He warns you that the plate is hot so don't touch it. You touch it anyway. The plate is so hot that you recoil, kicking into the table, which sends everything flying except for one small crumb from a breadstick. As you sit there blushing from the attention your ruckus has caused you hear a small voice. "Why oh why did you touch that hot plate?" the breadcrumb asks. You look down at the breadcrumb. You pick up the breadcrumb. You eat the breadcrumb. You burp with satisfaction and answer, "I wanted to be sure it was really there."

The senses that you possess while out of your body are primarily utilized by wanting to do so.

You want to 'see' so you see. You want to 'hear' so you hear. You want to 'smell' so you smell. Phew, I'll say. Go take a shower for goodness sake. These three senses translate over from the physical environment but are not quite the same. These nonphysical senses are guided by your selective perception and desire to make them work.

When traveling nonphysically in the physical environment you 'see' your garden by focusing on it to bring it to clarity. There will be a glow that permeates all that you see regardless of the actual light available. People may appear bathed in unexpected colors. You can see in the distance as sharply as close by.

When traveling nonphysically in the physical environment you desire to 'hear' the flapping of butterfly wings as one passes by, or the rumbling of thunder far away. You can hear distant sounds as clearly as close by.

When traveling nonphysically in the physical environment you want to 'smell' the flowers, drawing the scent into you. You can also smell a distant fire or that trash bin at the end of the block.

Once you've 'turned on' these three senses a few times it's not necessary to intentionally do so with each new out of body travel. As with all your nonphysical skills they are self-perpetuating once you're aware of them and have practiced a bit. It's like learning to walk. You no longer think about placing one foot in front of the other and balancing. You can just do it. You lift-out from your physical and you see right away. You want to look at the mountain a mile off and you do. You want to hear the neighbor's yelling and it happens. You want to smell that you still need a shower and I agree. Thankfully, scents are limited to the physical environment.

While nonphysical you may perceive sights and sounds that are either physical or nonphysical in nature. You may see and hear a mix of the two environments or just one or the other. This depends on the vibrational speed of your nonphysical body, which is guided by your desire.

TOUCHY TOUCHY

The fourth sense you possess while nonphysical is touch. You can 'touch' physical objects and also pass through them. You can feel each little bit of the physical object. You 'feel' the cold or heat or wet or dry of the physical environment all without discomfort. You can also touch nonphysical objects and, depending on your vibrational speed, pass through them. If the object is vibrating near or close to your own speed you may run into them. Not to worry as your nonphysical can't be hurt while traveling. It's a lot like bumper cars. There's the collision but it's a funny crash. Your sense of touch while nonphysical is automatic. Unlike sight and sound there's not a lot of practice required to realize that you've just plowed into a snowbank. You control the depth of this sense by moving more slowly through an object or by wanting to feel more closely of the object or environment.

TELL ME HOW YOU FEEL

Although you have no sense of taste while non-physical, as clearly stated by your wardrobe, I'm happy to report that there is another nonphysical sense to total five, just as your physical has. I wish I'd known about this sense before I was grabbed by Huggy Stuff because it would've saved me a lot of trouble.

When you're physical and you see me heading your way from up the block you have no idea what I'm up to. Am I going to push you out of my way? Am I going to give you a big hug? Am I going steal your bag of doughnuts and run off? You have no idea just what the heck I might do. But when you're nonphysical you have the sense of 'nonverbal communication'. You can 'feel' what another nonphysical traveler or entity is up to. You can sense if the nonphysical whatever is friendly or unfriendly. You can sense if they are happy or sad or angry or scared. You can even sense if they are sleeping, completely unaware that they are traveling nonphysically. You can sense all of this from a comfort zone that brings you nowhere near where they are. You don't even need to train yourself to do this. Just focus on the whatever it is and 'feel' what they are about. If it was Huggy Stuff you'd 'feel' its intent to grab and hang on, long before it reached you. If it's your neighbor overjoyed to see another traveler, you'd know it long before he's near enough to give you a big kiss. This advance warning gives you the opportunity to stay or leave. If you decide to stay you can still keep Huggy or your neighbor at bay by thinking 'stay away thoughts'. Only by ignoring or 'inviting' do you allow an intruder to overpower you. And even if that happens you can easily get away by thinking yourself back to your physical.

Your sense of nonverbal communication also allows you to exchange 'conversation' and thoughts with whatever you run into. You may either have normal conversations while nonphysical, 'sending' the words without actually speaking them, or you may 'send' a ball of information that takes place in a rapid-fire exchange of information that far exceeds normal conversation. You discern what's being 'sent' by the whatever and 'send' your own thoughts and feelings.

To explain the ball of information, when you're in your physical and you've just eaten a doughnut to end all doughnuts you would tell me about it with words. It was the most spectacular doughnut. It was a masterpiece. The filling was a delectable cream that danced on your tongue with pastry so light it practically floated into your mouth. The doughnut was drenched with blended chocolates yodeled from Switzerland and you've fallen in love with this confectionery delight. Okay, go buy some doughnuts before we go on with this example. You better save me one for when you get back.

Oh, you're back. Where's my doughnut? In your stomach. That's hilarious, wisenheimer. To continue, now that you're satiated, if I were to meet you while you were traveling and you wanted to brag about the doughnuts I could 'receive' all of your doughnut information, in all its sublime deliciousness, in one quick blip. I'd also receive the emotion you've attached to the doughnut and a 'visual' image of you snarfing it down. Our exchange would occur in a millisecond as opposed to minutes. Like throwing a compressed ball of information I would understand what you were 'sending' and you would understand what I sent.

To practice sending a ball of information think of something that you wish to convey. Rather than using words that describe it, use visual images to replace the words and concentrate on the feelings that surround your topic.

For example (times three):

➢ If you wanted to tell another traveler about your physical environment your visuals and feelings might include a clean clear lake, tall and lovely trees, you swaying happily in a hammock.

➢ If you wanted to tell another traveler about a cherished pet your visuals and feelings might include Fido chasing a stick, Fido chewing up your slippers, Fido cuddling in your lap, Fido wagging his tail in the next example.

➢ If you wanted to tell another traveler about your dinner your visuals and feelings might include a very hot plate of crunchy fish and chips, everything flying off the table except for one breadcrumb, burping with satisfaction, Fido enjoying the recovered flung food from a doggie bag.

Your intuition will serve you best for communicating during a travel. Although another traveler may only 'send' what he she or it wants you to receive, you can still discern if there's trouble to be avoided.

Read This If You Want

Somewhat demonstrative of nonverbal communication is the following diary entry. If I had known back then that I was going to write a book I'd have made it more interesting. Nonetheless (a word that has always fascinated me), this entry shows you something. Try to figure out what that something is and get back to me. I chopped out the really boring parts already so now it's only semi-boring.

August 2, 1986
Work was on my mind as I tried to become relaxed. I used travel suggestions and breathing techniques. I was at the entrance to Park 16 when six 'human' travelers floated towards me. There was some initial animosity on their part, which had overtones of race, but it passed almost immediately. We proceeded to 'chat' and I explained my job in the building, sending my thoughts and feelings as best I could.

During the group 'discussion' there was one among them who floated to the center and challenged me. The antagonist primarily used a threatening movement to do so. It was quickly realized that I wouldn't rise to the aggressive level being exhibited and our exchange of nonphysical attack and counter-attack was then carried out in good humor. Rough housing is the best way to describe it. This was followed by a short bit of further discussion and then I returned to the physical.

Wow. I can't believe you read that whole thing. I hope that showed you something. Something like nonverbal communication comes naturally as one of your nonphysical senses. You can enjoy your encounters with others that you meet and protect yourself when you need to. Something like that.

KNOW IT ALL

Did you know that you can touch, see, hear, and smell while nonphysical? Did you also know that you have the sense of nonverbal communication? You're like a superhero. A superhero who read the last few chapters and a superhero who can do other neat stuff like the following.

While nonphysical you can pass through a rocky mountain or a giant pile of feathers placed just so. You can go underwater or into space without running out of oxygen or blowing up. I just made myself queasy. Extremes of weather and temperature are experienced without discomfort. Faraway places are within your traveling distance. You can go anywhere you want, superhero.

All superheroes have their weaknesses and you're no exception. You can't move physical objects while nonphysical. If you do move something physically, it's by force of will not by nonphysical contact.

Physical folks and Fido can see you there, flying in your super cape. Under the right lighting, which is dim and from behind, you can attract the attention of someone or more likely an animal to your presence. You may also 'touch' the person or pet. This is likely to make any species jump so you must decide if this is funny or inappropriate. Right, I'll just put you down for 'funny'. So I take it back, you *can* move something physical while nonphysical. But they won't like it.

The nonphysical speed that you initially vibrate at while traveling is only slightly faster than that of the physical, so you overlap and perceive both environments. But after a while of super-heroing around the physical environment you might want to increase your vibrational speed and move to environments less connected, or completely separate, from the physical. Nothing is stopping you. Your desire to speed up the vibe is all it takes. You'll see one environment shimmer away and the higher vibrating environment take its place.

As a superhero your shape while nonphysical can be anything at all or almost nothing. You initially choose a human physical shape because that's what you know. But when I tell you to wave your arms, they could just as well be the shape of tiger paws or eagle talons. Your entire form is based on what you want and what's required for the environment you're visiting. Your nonphysical size is also decided by you. If you need to get through a pinhole, you can. Your consciousness doesn't require a vessel to travel here or there, mostly there. When you reach the very fastest vibrating environments there isn't a nonphysical at all. It's just you as a superhero dot of consciousness.

STEP SEVEN: RETURN AND MEMORY

PHYSICALLY ATTRACTED TO YOU

While you're doing all this traveling about in your nonphysical it should comfort you to know that you are still connected to your physical body by a 'rubber-band'. There are many names for this connection to your physical but this is my jargon-free choice. Even when you're a dot of consciousness you're not separated from the snoozy-you back in bed. This 'rubber-band' is a wonderful safeguard, albeit somewhat annoying at times.

Unlike a normal rubber-band this one pulls back with less force the farther you stretch it. If you're a thousand miles away it's not likely to bounce you back to your physical without your conscious or subconscious direction. When the band is at its smallest however, connecting your nonphysical to your physical by a matter of inches, the band has a stronger pull that can easily yank you back into bed. The pull can be overwhelming despite your resolve to stay nonphysical. This is why you should move away quickly following lift-out.

The rubber-band insures that you will never get lost while nonphysically traveling. It's better than a trail of bread and considerably less crummy. When you want to return to your physical you only have to think of your physical body. You feel for it and reach for it and tell yourself to go back. The rubber-band pulls you back neat and tidy, re-aligning your nonphysical with your physical, often in reverse of the way you lifted-out. You can also return slower, meandering along the way, and still benefit from the rubber-band's guidance, confident that you will always know where you last left you. This is done by first concentrating on the direction of your physical body and then moving towards your physical with a controlled dilly-dally attitude. You simply instruct yourself to return at a pace of your choosing.

The rubber-band also alerts you and pulls you back in response to any event that involves your physical, such as the dog sleeping on your head.

Your return to your physical is much easier than getting out because it's your natural state of being. You live in a physical environment so your physical takes precedence over your nonphysical. Being nonphysical is the oddity, requiring more effort to push beyond your normal physical perspective.

SHORT TERM MEMORY LOSS IS A ...

I've covered the importance of imprinting your nonphysical travel to physical memory after you return. It was way back at the beginning of the book so you might have forgotten by now. But if you forget to remember about remembering memories they should cancel each other out and then you'd remember to remember and ... oh forget it. I'm getting a headache just trying to remember what my point was before I forgot.

I don't have anything to add to what I said earlier since it was perfect the first time. So here's a rerun because memory is the second part of Step Seven. The first part of Step Seven was a Return to your physical. You just read how easy that is in the last chapter but have probably forgotten that by now.

A clean memory of the nonphysical event requires that it be imprinted upon the physical brain, immediately upon return. A simple conscious effort to recall the nonphysical event, after returning to the physical, is enough to imprint the travel. If the return to the physical is followed instead by falling directly to sleep, without committing the event from nonphysical knowledge to physical knowledge, there's a good chance of a muddled memory later or none at all of the event.

To Travel For Example

The following is a mix-match of various diary entries I've made over the years to demonstrate how a potential travel might play out for you. It contains most of what I've yapped about up until this point. Change whatever I do to something you would do and change any of my events to events that you can relate to. By the time you're done, this entry should be considerably more interesting.

Nonever 33, 2011
I was hopeful for some traveling last night after my long day of writing. To prepare for this nonphysical agenda I took a bike ride to tire myself physically. I followed this with a hot shower in the dark to calm my thoughts.

As I relaxed in bed I planned my nonphysical travel. I decided to visit my old neighborhood back in Maryland. Since it's a long way off from where I live now I planned to first lift-out and go to the nearby gazebo. From there I would then direct a quick travel to the old neighborhood rather than meandering all the way. Then I'd tool around the neighborhood and the woods where I played as a somewhat younger me.

My relaxation method soon brought me to the awake/asleep line. I felt a surge so I spun-out and flew through my bedroom window to the grass below. It was a moonless night but everything shimmered with the glow of being nonphysical.

I moved away quickly and headed for the gazebo. There I spied the big and mouthy duck I raised, BooBoo. I didn't want to frighten her so I kept my distance. I felt for the old neighborhood and quickly began to move in that direction. I enjoyed the incredible speed of the travel. After about ten seconds I began to slow. I came to float about fifteen feet above the ground in the backyard of where I grew up. Talk about a good landing.

I took off exploring as I'd planned to do. I flew through the woods and up the near-vertical trail I'd climbed on my way to high school. I ventured to the creek and rocks where I'd hung out on summer nights. I went over my street and took it to the end where it emptied onto the main roads. There were new buildings where the woods had been and shopping centers and lots of parked cars. At last I visited my elementary school playground. I explored the large, open-air, upper level. I then rose to a few hundred feet and scanned the neighborhood.

I decided it was time to return so I felt for the direction to travel and slowly moved towards my physical. After a bit I allowed the speed to increase gradually until it blurred and I was soon near my home again. I saw another traveler outside my complex but I couldn't discern any intentional messages being sent. I sent a brief greeting but avoided an invitation due to that lack of communication. It seemed they were not aware that they were traveling and only dreaming their actions. I moved off to below my bedroom window and floated gently up. I went back through the glass and spun-in, in reverse of the way I'd left. I could feel the 'charge' throughout my body that often remains a few minutes after return. I lay quietly thinking about my travel, committing it to my physical memory for a later entry.

Extra Extra Read All About It

Now that you understand how to travel non-physically, and what to expect while out, I'm going to toss more thoughts and methods your way to give you a broader knowledge of the experience. A few of the following chapters require you to take an extra leap of faith to believe because they are so unusual. If you decide not to take that leap, that's dandy. If I had not personally experienced what I'm going to tell you I might not believe me either. We'll start slow, with belief itself.

Reasoning From A Circle

As children we accept that things exist simply because they seem to. This creates a perpetual motion of belief and a fulfillment of that belief. It was this circle of belief that led me forward to where I am today, sitting in a uncomfortable chair and writing about my nonphysical obsession.

As a child I quickly accepted that I could get out of my physical body. There were no good explanations offered to disprove my odd events so I went with the obvious reality. And when I accepted the nonphysical without question there was nothing to stop me from experiencing it.

I believed the late night out of body travels to my neighbor's home. I believed the flights across my school playground. I believed the sunny mornings floating in the front yard. I was not in my bed. I was out of body. Because I believed, the circle carried me forward and around to discover it.

To remind you of the importance of belief in the nonphysical write the following on your bathroom mirror as I just did. I used a lipstick marker, or whatever women call those things. No, it was not *my* lipstick. It wasn't. Shut up, you. It was *not* mine. Although I did like the color. Hmm, maybe a little blush too and... never mind.

"Belief equals Acceptance equals Traveling."

The nonphysical environment is similar to seeing a shadow that's reflected onto a wall in very dim light. The shadow is there although it's hard to see at first. It is slowly revealed as your eyes want to adjust, allowing you to perceive that it exists.

Traveling is unusual. All of your experiences leading up to a travel, and the travel itself, do not fit into the norm. But just because something is different from what you expect does not make that something any less important or less real than your normal somethings. It's just unknown for now.

Take Off

There are some folks willing to sell you a nonphysical experience. They sell gizmos and hype. It's almost like buying a plane ticket.

"Step up to the ticket counter please." The clerk is speaking to you. "Yes you, next please. Hurry it along." You move forward and request information on getting out of your body. "Well, as you can see, we offer many different options for your nonphysical flight dependent on your cash flow. You say you can only afford business class? In that case we will accept your money now and later, when you have more money, we will upgrade your ticket so that you can have even better experiences." You pay the money you have to the clerk and receive your ticket. You read the fine print on the back. "All tickets and upgrades are non-refundable. All fees are also non-refundable regardless of whether you leave your body or not." You sigh and tear up the worthless ticket. You then realize that you have imagined the whole incident and that I am yapping on about something. You must have zoned out.

My friend, there is only one way to travel beyond your body. You must *want* to travel. Knowing the basics is plenty and everything beyond that is a distraction. Gizmos and hype, and even this author, are just tickets to get you where you can already go. Watch your wallet and don't fall for the overpriced tickets that claim they can launch you from your body. Just because the plane looks new and fancy doesn't mean it flies. Adapt anything that you learn about traveling nonphysically to fit your way of thinking. Don't allow outside influences to become the center of your traveling. You can already travel.

PUDDING PROOF

In your early attempts at traveling you may wish to confirm that you're nonphysical just to prove it to yourself. Confirmation is accomplished by examining this and that while nonphysical, and then checking on what you observed when you return to your physical. Here are some confirmation examples.

To quickly confirm that you're nonphysical, look at a clock. A digital clock is easiest to read while traveling and having it in another room is a plus. Set the time on the clock by pressing the buttons without looking at it. Then, when you're out of body, get a very exact reading from the clock and immediately zip back to your physical. Now get up and check that clock! The clock should be no more than a minute off from what you expect.

For confirmation of a place or event, you non-physically visit a nearby location that is unfamiliar or only vaguely familiar. You examine tiny details of the area that would normally go unnoticed. You observe events that may be occurring while you're there. Later, you visit the location physically, assuming that you have a general idea of where in heck the place is, and do a physical follow up by comparing what you noted while nonphysical.

You can check on your partner if you're in bed and they're not. Go look in on them. What are they up to? Try to note something that they're doing that's different from their routine as you expect it. It might be a small detail like they brush their teeth up and down rather than side to side. When you get back to your physical confirm your findings. After they stop laughing at you they may actually believe you, but don't count on it. I should have warned you sooner that perception is in the eye of the beholder. Proving your travels to someone else is just a waste of time. Just because you have conclusive evidence of your nonphysical events doesn't mean that others will find your rationale the least bit plausible. Belief proves nothing except to ourselves. If you're convinced, that's all that matters.

More Desirable

Without Desire there is no out of body. The event will escape you. This is a shame because Desire is your buddy. So say, "Hey there, Desire. How are you doing?" And Desire will say, "Stop talking to me. I'm only a concept, you rube."

Desire is easy to work with. Use desire to think outward, into the next step of your traveling. That is what desire is. It is the next thing that you want. Desire is the next thing that you want. Yes, you just read that a second ago. You have a good memory.

You get a signal that your nonphysical is ready to lift-out. Desire to be by your chair in the living room. You're there. Desire to be in the garden. You're there. Desire to be up over your house. You're there. Desire to find Aunt Gladys. She's hiding money behind the medicine cabinet again. Desire to catch her in the act. You're there in a blink. Traveling is many desired actions, one to the next. That is how you get out of body and that is how you stay out of body.

CONFESSIONAL

Hello. My name is Alan Guiden and I travel. While my neighbors sleep I am busily jumping in and out of my physical body. What's that? You already know that I travel? Well then, you must not be my neighbor. My neighbors don't know of my odd forte. They don't know that I am floating over their familiar streets. They don't know that I am visiting amazing and remote places. In short, too late, they simply have no idea of what I do. They probably don't even know what traveling is. Or maybe they do.

Why should I assume that my neighbors don't travel? It's possible that they know all about traveling. It's possible they have read my book. They just don't know it's me living nearby because we never talk about traveling. It doesn't come up in conversation. If they're interested in traveling we'd have a fine chat. But if they're not interested they'd say I'm an annoying kook. So who do we, who are interested in traveling, talk to? Before the Internet the answer was no one. It was very rare to find another person to discuss the topic. With the Internet we have an unlimited ability to communicate with others of similar interests. You can yap to your heart's content with folks just like yourself without being personally identified. One outlet for Internet communication is "out of body" bulletin boards. You can post messages to these bulletin boards and read the posts of others. By talking about traveling you increase your chances of doing it because your thoughts are centered upon it.

The Number One Two-Part Question

I receive a lot of fan email. Yes, I find it hard to believe too. Most of the time the emails are a combination of rump-kissing and questions. The number one two-part question is included in the following actual email. I deleted the rump-kissing part already. You're welcome.

Dear Mr. Guiden,

After reading your website I managed to have two travels last week but I have had nothing since. I'm doing all the same things but it's not working. I feel frustrated. What am I doing wrong, and does this ever happen to you?

Dear Whoever You Are,

Thank you for writing. Please include your name next time so that I know what to call you. For now, I'll call you Teddy. Your family history is a long line of stuffed toy bears.

That's a great question that you ask, Teddy. Let me answer the second part of your question first and then work back to the first part that then actually becomes the second part. That'll teach you for sending me email. Does a lack of traveling success ever happen to me, THE GREAT ALAN GUIDEN? Could I, the expert's expert, have gone for periods in which I did not travel at all despite my very best efforts? Could I, the oh so awesome, super-talented star of traveling, get out of body many many times one week but none the next? Ummm, *yes*. I'm actually just like you, Teddy. Of course I've been struck by this phenomenon. I call it 'the lull factor'. The lull factor is the time between the last really cool thing that happened to you non-physically and the next really cool thing that happens.

The lull could be a few days, a few weeks, or longer. You try this you try that and nothing happens. Do you want my advice, Teddy? Nod your fluffy head. My advice is don't let the lulls get to you. Before long you'll have another travel to call your last travel before the last lull which had three travels before that lull and those really nifty travels before that previous lull. It's the ups and downs of the sport.

Please repeat this out loud so as to instruct your neighbors: My attempts at non-physical traveling will be great and less great. Sometimes I will, sometimes I won't, but I can only get better no matter how long it takes.

Just keep at it and don't get discouraged, Teddy. As toy bears go, you take the stuffing.

Yours sincerely,
Alan Guiden

Dear Mr. Guiden,

I don't understand why you felt the need to say that I "take the stuffing" near the end of your email. That's a big insult to a toy bear. You are obviously not familiar with the great stuffing uprising of '93. You need to stop writing so much and do a little reading. Otherwise, thanks for the reply.

Teddy

Planning Is Doing

Plan your travel. Plan your travel. I can't say it enough. Have a plan of what you are going to do when you're nonphysical. Have a plan that puts you where you want to be. Any small plan is better than none to maintain your control and awareness while traveling.

For an instance of an example to be examined, let's plan for some California waves, shall we? Nod your platinum-blond head of hair, *yes*.

Your plan includes your lift-out and you'll go right through your roof. Then you'll zip on up to five thousand feet to get your bearings and head west. Next, you'll hold your arms out in front of you, because it's a super sight-gag, and off you'll fly to the beach.

It's easy to make a plan for your traveling. It starts with your desire to be someplace or do something. Keep your plan in your thoughts and expect the experience to happen. Be creative and be adaptive. Rotate your plans. Try one plan a few nights and then try a different one. Create new plans based on what you've learned from past plans.

Balancing Act

Happy circus music begins to play. *Do Doo Do Doo Do Do Do Doo Do Do.* Some joyful clowns tumble out of a small car, toss a few pies, and then assemble a see-saw in the center ring.

I step out, full of bravado in a dark blue tux, and begin waving my arms wildly while shouting this and that into a microphone. But you can't hear me because an elephant has trampled the sound booth. I pick up a megaphone instead. "NOW presenting in the center ring... One of my favorite ways to reach the awake/asleep line!" The crowd gets all excited and spills their popcorn. The front row is caught in the avalanche. They eat their way out and the concession stands make a big score in soda pop sales. When everyone has calmed down you look to the center ring with its clown-built see-saw. It is then that you realize the see-saw is just like the awake/asleep. One side is the awake side and the other side is the asleep side. The see-saw is balanced so that both sides can remain off the ground at once, but it is a precarious balance not easily centered. The see-saw may move slightly down on one side and up on the other. It can be balanced by pushing down on the up side, but not too much push or you'll need to recorrect. You must shift the weight gently and watch for changes of one side or the other moving off balance to find the center of the see-saw.

Congratulations. You and the clowns have just managed an image of the awake/asleep line. Like the see-saw, you will find that your balance on the awake/asleep line is a matter of a few degrees this way or that. If you maintain this imagery you should find that you reach the line without any direct concentration upon doing so. The image and symbolism of the see-saw, or any similar balancing concept that pleases you, imprints itself upon your subconscious as a desire to remain in control. You are telling yourself to stay centered and balanced on the line. This allows your physical to go one way in its need for sleep, while you go another way in your need for traveling.

Read My Thoughts

I've been logging my out of body travels for a long time. In the beginning I wrote in a small blue diary. Next it was composition books. Then a cassette recorder. After that it was a micro-cassette recorder, a typewriter, a word processor, a desktop computer, a laptop, a hand-held PC, and back to a recorder once they went digital. I have written and recorded my traveling thoughts all over the place. But I almost never share those words in my work and here's the reason. I feel that my travels are of most value when taken as a whole to explain the process. My singular events are not as important as the basic how-tos I can take from them to help you learn to travel. Nonetheless, many readers have written asking to read more of my ditties. So I will now share with you seven entries spanning a brief period of time.

In these entries I travel to ancient Babylonia and rescue the queen. That's a joke. You are so gullible. The queen was quite capable of rescuing herself. Actually, I chose these entries because they are not astounding. These entries are just average events that you may experience in your attempts to travel. That's what makes these entries better than any tale I could tell you about meeting the Digsunes deep down in the earth's core. That's another joke. Digsunes don't care much for hot spots. Unlike those bad jokes, I do have interesting travels to relate to you that really happened. I'll tell you two of those soon. For now, though, I'll share a month of typical traveling.

Let's hop in our time machine and dial the start date to:

October 28, 1994
Last night was mostly sleepless except for a few busy dreams which contained part

thoughts about writing and part junk from earlier in the evening. At 4:30am, on my right side and with thoughts of traveling prevalent, I had a right to left slide-out from physical to the edge of the bed and a brief trip to the door of the bedroom. It was smooth and I didn't feel vibrations. I don't recall any other details but with my lack of sleep that was probably it anyhow.

November 1, 1994
I awoke last night about 2:30 and, after tending for a few moments to some cat shenanigans in the kitchen, I returned to bed with a desire to get out. I tried my right side for about forty minutes and then switched to my left side. After about ten minutes I was out. I moved to the front of the bed and floated about, attempting to awaken my girlfriend but she continued to sleep. I then went out the bedroom screen-window and after visiting the gazebo, per my earlier instructions, I took off in a west and slightly north direction.

I noticed a deep blue-green tinge to the night sky as I traveled. As the flight continued I observed to my right, a small steep mountain area with flat cliffs jutting out. There was grass growing on the cliffs and scattered about on the mountain. I had been experiencing duality during the majority of the trip and eventually allowed myself to pull back to physical. The arm I was laying on was suffering some discomfort which was the reason for my call to return. It was 3:37am. I noted a slight charge and minor vibrations upon return.

November 5, 1994

I woke at about 3:30am and was intent upon getting out. I lay on my right side and waited to relax again. After about a half hour I had a bit of trouble breathing through my nose but rather than rouse myself I breathed through my mouth. I eventually slid out right to left and went through my bedroom door and moved down the hallway. I thought of my physical due to my breathing difficulty and returned. There was no pressing problem so I went back through the door and went out the living room window. I landed gently among the square trimmed bushes which are just below the window and then meandered around the stream and gazebo area for a few minutes. I looked up to admire the moon and stars. My return to physical was sooner than I would have liked but again I must blame my slight breathing difficulty for the urge to pull back.

November 8, 1994

I awoke at approximately 3:00am and was ready to travel as usual. After about twenty minutes on my back I had a dream which went on for awhile. At some point I realized I was dreaming and immediately regained full consciousness. I was already out but initially at a loss as to my location. I floated past a hedge of some kind, went through and entered a garden behind a home. Then I knew I was in the French quarter. The hidden gardens off the street from view are popular as tours but I've never taken one. The garden was beautiful and lush with scented flowers everywhere and two cats laying about. A sprinkler popped on. It felt delightful floating there as the water fell. I was able to also discern the coolness of the air. I was thinking to myself how great the whole experience was. The travel lasted about fifteen minutes and then I returned to physical. Time check was 3:57am.

November 12, 1994

After a few hours sleep from approximately 10pm to 2am, I stayed awake in bed thinking this and that. Eventually I was relaxed enough to concentrate on traveling. I planned a route and lay on my right side. The night was quite a bit warmer than it usually is this time of year. I had trouble getting comfortable in the heavy blanket which was useful a few nights ago. At about 4:00am I experienced strong but irregular vibe and, although I attempted to calm the vibe, my effort was not adequate. I let the vibe fade, still glad to have experienced it as a reward for my efforts.

November 23, 1994

I've been slightly annoyed with myself for not getting out lately. It's actually only been a couple of weeks according to my entries but it's frustrating. However, last night I did have a travel that helped to calm me down.

I was laying on my left side and finally relaxed enough to touch the awake/asleep line. I felt a surge signal building so I immediately attempted lift-out. I also had a mild pseudo interruption just prior to actually lifting-out. I recognized it as such and pushed it away from my thoughts as unreal.

I went out the bedroom window, taking time to observe the venetian blind which was halfway drawn over the screen as I passed through. I set down amid some gardening tools which were surprisingly below my window. The maintenance man must have left them. I later verified they were actually there after my return to physical.

My vision was clear and I was quite happy just to be out enjoying the nighttime air and moonlit sky. Upon return I had a brief psi-headache which usually means I forced a lift-out too quickly rather than wait for the conditions to reach optimum. Time check was 3:07am.

December 1, 1994

I want to remember this small event. A travel took place just this morning that reminded me it's always the little things that make traveling so much fun. I had not pre-planned a travel prior to my lift-out so I ran a route that I often do while physical. I visited the balcony to check out the ducks. As expected, my flock of feathered friends were quacking underneath the balcony. But what I realize now is that my vantage was different from when I visit the balcony physically. I had a completely unobstructed view of the ducks even though they were almost directly under me, which means that I was above the railing and slightly away from the balcony. It's so natural to be above the ground while non-physical that, instead of my normal vantage at the balcony, I was five feet up. I would never have considered physically climbing up higher and over the railing to watch the ducks. But I just safely put a ladder out on the balcony to recreate the vantage point. It's wild to see something physically—when the only time you've previously seen it or done it was nonphysically.

Duality Dance

Your consciousness may exist in many places at the same time and this is not unusual. It's *not*, I say. Even during your normal waking state you may be in two or more places at the same time. It's your selective perception that decides which place will get the majority of your attention.

You're sitting in your chair watching television but you're thinking towards the refrigerator for a cold drink. You see yourself going to the fridge. You get to the fridge. You're now inside the fridge, standing on a lettuce leaf. Any drinks left in there? Get me one while you're at it. *Ta da!* You just existed in the fridge *and* in your chair at the same time. Your perception made it happen.

While nonphysical you may experience duality, or even triality, due to your ability to perceive more than one event and place. It's just like being in class. There's the teacher speaking but you also hear doodling pencils and classmates snoring and you see the lovely day beyond the window and look at the bird on the tree singing a tune and the snap of a ruler on your butt and you're back to answering questions at the blackboard. *Ta da!* You just did it again. Your perception makes it possible to be many places at once.

You may perceive both your physical in bed and your nonphysical in Antarctica. You can see and feel your physical resting comfortably, so there's no need to rush back from your conversation with that penguin. You've been using selective perception your whole life to put your consciousness in multiple places. This is not unusual. It's *not*, I say.

SOUND ADVICE

I am now going to share a method with you for reaching the awake/asleep line that I had completely forgotten about. I had used this method over and over in my early traveling with great success. But treating this method like an old toy, I placed it in a metaphorical box way back in the closet. Then one day I found it again while looking for a metaphorical shirt to wear that still had buttons.

My last night was probably just like yours, ordinary. The particulars of my quiet evening were a movie with dinner and then some nice music as I prepared for bed. It was just another night of winding down. Suddenly without warning, which is the only way suddenly happens, a commercial came on to interrupt my music. This was soon followed by another commercial and yet another and another and AAAAAHHHhhh!!! There are just too many commercials. Why, I never in my whole life have heard so much... oh wait, I was supposed to tell you a method. Why do you let me prattle on?

Everyone has a few songs that really get them going. Your songs might be from a musical, or a hit on the radio, or a classical piece, or a television show. Next time you're ready to go traveling choose a selection from your personal jukebox. Pick any song that relaxes and pleases you. Now put on a headset and listen to the song two times in a row. Tired of it yet? Too bad, listen one more time before taking off the headset. The song is in your recent memory now. It likes it in there. You can recall every nuance and note as you lay there relaxing. Allow the song to play in your thoughts and gain strength from the details in your memory. As you focus you can hear the song from everywhere. With each spin of your selection you highlight more points of music and sound. You quickly reach a deep concentration. While this is occurring, the calming effect of your focus soon has your physical sleeping. You may become so wrapped up in your selection, as you reach the awake/asleep line, that the only signal of your arrival to the line may be that your selection seems to be playing extremely loud. As if you are standing next to concert hall speakers, the music will envelop you. This is your musical cue to get out of your body. Put your travel plan immediately into action and slide from your body. Down the hall. You're going down the hall. Passing through the front door. You're outside. You're moving up the street. Go, Go, Go!

QUESTIONS AND ANSWERS

Do you fear leaving your physical body? Do you fear what you might run into out there in the nonphysical? Do you fear falling from nonphysical flight and that you'll get hurt when you hit the ground? Do you fear that you will get lost from your physical? Do you fear that you won't get back into your physical? Do you fear that someone will think you're dead while you're away from your physical? Do you fear that something creepy will take over your physical while you're gone? Do you fear that traveling will make you miss an important physical event that requires your attention? Do you fear the unknown? Well, *don't*.

Your physical body will be perfectly fine while you are away from it. Other travelers that you may meet are more interesting than frightening. You can't fall from nonphysical flight without a conscious or subconscious desire to do so and it doesn't hurt even a little bit if you do. You can always find your way back and get into your physical because you are connected to your physical. Any outside observer can tell that your physical body is sleeping. Your physical body is your body and nothing else gets in it. You may be easily called back to your physical by any outside event that involves your physical. Never fear the unknown because it's only unknown until you get to know it.

Emotion Explosion

It's often difficult to remain calm while nonphysical but still near your physical body. The overwhelming excitement is due in part to the actual *incredibleness* of the event. So what, if that's not a word? It's a thrill to realize that you're nonphysical so of course you're excited. But emotional highs and lows are also affected by your nonphysical proximity to your physical body. When you are in near-sync to your physical, emotions may amplify without restraint. While this is good for an abundance of happy, it's bad for emotions like fear. A brush with amplified fear can easily drag you right back into yourself. There doesn't even need to be a cause for the alarm. One second you're wary and the next second you're terrified and the next second you're back in your physical. So until you're seasoned enough, with salt and pepper, move quickly away from your physical. The emotional boost will fade as you put some distance between the two of your bodies, allowing you to travel more rationally.

Knock Knock Who's There Go Away

I have received emails regarding the possibility of being "possessed" while physical or nonphysical and I just want to say this about that: When was the last time you spoke with a possessed person? I'm not talking about some gal who seems a bit daft or a guy who needs serious medical attention, I'm talking *possession*. It's just not happening. Despite hype about the dangers of something invading your physical body or being taken over while nonphysical, it's not happening. The only way something gets hold of your goodies even temporarily, as with "channeling", is if you want it to.

It's *your* physical body and you are connected to it. It's a sealed connection. The door is locked tight. Nothing gets in without your say-so. Just as you protect your physical in your waking life to look out for that bus, you protect it during sleep. It's automatic. Nothing kicks you out of your own physical or takes your nonphysical from you. Don't worry about something wanting your bodies. That only happens in Hollywood.

A Ghost Story

Nonphysical traveling has influenced my belief in life after death. It's not the same thing, but it does point to its existence. A travel is more than a psi-related event. The consciousness exists beyond the body. Therefore, the question regarding death is where does the consciousness *go*?

For a time when I was a teen I became interested in thoughts of assisting others while I was nonphysical. My desire was to be useful with my odd ability. The way it turned out, I did indeed visit those who seemed in need of my counsel. These visits included a travel to a downtrodden gent whose small novelty store was going under; a travel to a woman whose biggest concern was her fancy-schmancy dinner party; and the following travel, which really surprised me.

It was late afternoon when I was drawn out of body to a young woman's home. She sat on a couch by the window. She sat very quietly, wringing her hands. She was also nonphysical. After a bit, she looked up at me as if I had been there all along and she spoke. The woman asked if I would speak with her brother in the next room. She said that she needed him to leave her house. She said that she loved him but that he had been there for such a long time she couldn't bring herself to tell him. I agreed to speak with him.

I entered the next room and saw the brother upon his bed. He was sitting up with his back to a large pillow but he looked uncomfortable. He was asleep and in the physical yet I spoke to him anyway. "Your sister would like you to leave now. She loves you but she says it's time to go." The sleeping brother slid just a bit out of his physical, looking drawn and tired. I continued: "Your sister wants her home back. She can't bring herself to ask you but she wants you to please leave now." With those words the brother slowly poured out onto the floor. I watched as his nonphysical collected itself. He then headed for the far wall and went through, exiting the house. I followed, leaving his physical behind.

After a short time the brother and I reached a large pasture. I didn't recognize the area but it seemed that he did. He stopped and turned to face me. He said four words: "I love my sister." Then he vibed right past my perception. A quick shimmer and he was gone.

Following the brother's quick departure I returned to the home of the sister. I really had no idea what I had just done or witnessed. It seemed to me that the brother had simply traveled off to somewhere else for a while, but would be returning eventually. Although this was possible, it was not as I thought.

The woman was still nonphysical upon the couch and nonphysical tears fell from her face. She said that she could feel that her brother was gone. Again, I didn't understand, for he was still in the next room, physically upon the bed. She sensed my confusion and tried to explain. She told me that she felt so awful for her brother and that she felt guilty. After all, her brother was dying. He needed her care. But the burden of caring for him was too great. It had gone on for so many years. She felt her life was slipping away with his. She wanted her brother at peace and she wanted to live again. Through me, she said, she had saved them both. Then I realized what I had done. Without understanding the situation I had convinced her brother to take a nonphysical travel, *permanently*. I had convinced him to die.

Okay, so that's not really a ghost story. I never got to see the ghost of her brother. There wasn't any haunting or ectoplasmic glop. But I was as shocked as if you'd just yelled *BOO!* I had no idea that when I asked her brother to leave it meant forever. So, back to the first paragraph of this no-ghost story, the question regarding death is where does the consciousness go? It's my opinion, which means nothing, that the brother went to where the consciousness goes for a while when the physical gives out. I don't know where that place is for him but that's where he went. And he'll be back. It's like getting a new car. There's the time between selling your old car and getting the new car when you don't have a car. It could be a few seconds or days or weeks or years. You're just you, existing without a car until the new model comes out. But I'm just guessing.

Planetary Prose

The following is a dramatization based on complete fact. Only the words have been changed from the original dull diary entry to prevent you from falling asleep. Play some spacey jazz music while reading the following.

I was a bit concerned about my intention to fly around Mars, more because of the sheer distance in physical terms than the extreme physical conditions of space. Of course I had no need to fear either, as I would be nonphysical at the time, but some habits are hard to shake. I pushed my misplaced apprehension aside. A travel such as this required focus and worries just get in the way. I'd heard the story on the radio, so I wasn't really sure what the "face" looked like that I was going to see. But I figured I could spot it if there was such a thing.

When the hour struck four I touched off for the red planet. The trip was quick, but not so quick as a spin around the block. Still, I flew through the system in a matter of minutes and there I was, soaring very high above Mars. I began to move in a slow roll across its surface. After about ten minutes of enjoying the scenery on my leisurely flight, I suddenly saw the face. It slid into my view from the edge of the planet as I moved forward. There it was. A face. There was a face on Mars. No doubt about it. I needed a closer look.

Down down down I went, which took all of three seconds. The face began to lose definition. Down and down. The face began to look more like rocks and more rocks. Down down down down. Now the face was gone. So up up up up I went and then up up and up up up. I counted the ups and downs. And the face was back. Once again, down times nine I went and there was no face. So uppity up I went and there it was again. And do you know what I think about the face on Mars?

Big Pause. (Tie your shoelaces or something.)

It's my conclusion that someone has rearranged, set-up, manipulated or maneuvered that section of Mars terrain to make it look like a face. I know there are skeptics and scientists who have done their best to discern that it's just a bunch of rocks in the right lighting but to me the face looks intentional. Yes, at ground level it's not so impressive — but from above, as the designers would have intended it to be viewed, it's some mighty fine handy work mixed with a good dose of environmental chaos. That's my two trillion cents opinion. Space exploration is expensive work.

COMPLICATION SITUATION

It occurs to me, not for the first time, that traveling beyond my physical body is a gift that I gave to myself. For although my early traveling leaped out from behind the curtain shouting "Surprise!", it would not have continued to unwrap without my direct involvement.

It was due to my intense interest to understand this spontaneous gift that I was led to a hodge-podge of discoveries that soon became the basis for my attempts to control it. It wasn't long (unlike that last sentence), before I began to notice that not every part that led up to a nonphysical travel needed to be perceived for the travel to happen. In other words (because these words would like a bit of fame too), sometimes you will jump from one part of traveling to another without noticing the entire process. I first discovered this while playing with the vibration signal that may be experienced prior to a lift-out from the physical body.

At age eleven I had been working with an idea for 'waving' the vibe up and down my body, in an attempt to smooth out the spikes for lift-out, when suddenly the vibration disappeared completely. Poof and gone. So there I am, wanting to travel as my physical snoozed upon the bed, but with no vibe. What can I do? Whatever can I do?! Play some dramatic music here. Should I break the focus of my efforts and call it a night? Should I try to restart the vibration? Should I target all of my thoughts into 'feeling' the vibe again? Well, I'll tell you what I do, err... *did*. I got up for a glass of water. I decided that if I didn't feel vibration there was no reason to attempt a jump out of my body and opted instead for some liquid refreshment.

As I was heading for the door of my room I felt an abrupt tug at my back. At first, since I was groggy, I attempted to ignore this pull and continue in my path. However after a few seconds of annoyance I was forced to turn around so that I might find what it was that I had caught myself in. The next thing I saw was my physical coming up fast as I catapulted towards it, end over end from across the room. *BLAM!* In a flash I was re-synced with my body. I immediately jumped up thinking I was still nonphysical, but once again this was the opposite of my circumstances and I fell physically to the floor in a pile of blankets.

While you may find my fall to the floor funny, I can't let your laughter at my expense sidetrack the point of this chapter, which I have since forgotten, but I'll check my notes... Humm humm hummm. Oh yes. *Do not over-complicate your traveling attempts.*

As it turns out, the reason I could no longer feel the vibration was that it had already increased in speed beyond my present level of perception. This made it appear that the vibe had vanished when in fact the vibe was at an optimum rate for sliding out of my body. This taught me the following things. It is not necessary to feel vibration or any other signals before you get out of your body. You may move smoothly from physical sleep to separation without passing every checkpoint on your way there. Don't over-complicate the process of traveling. Don't get bogged down with why this or that did or didn't happen. Your determined alertness and a desire-driven plan to be elsewhere is all you need. Falling out of bed is funnier when it happens to someone else.

Take A Guess At Least

While we're here anyway, visiting the basics of being nonphysical, here's a quick quiz to test what you've learned.

The spotlights come up. The curtain parts. I step out onto the stage. I am momentarily dazzled by the lights and walk into the podium, which falls over along with all my notes. I make a graceless recovery. "Welcome my friends to another exciting round of *Travel Tricks!*" Impressive win-a-lot-of-prizes-music begins to play. "Yes, *Travel Tricks!* The exciting game where you learn how to leave your physical body! I'm your host, Alan Guiden. Let's get right to it, shall we?"

1. Anyone with a strong, focused desire can travel beyond their physical body. (This is an easy one.)
   ➢ True
   ➢ False

2. For a clean memory of your nonphysical travel you should...
> Wash your brain.
> Make a conscious effort to recall the event as soon as you return to your physical.
> Repeat the phrase, "I remember, I remember" seven times.
> Quickly tell someone else about the event.

3. The 'awake/asleep line' is...
> The joining between the here-now reality and other nonphysical environments.
> The moment just before your alarm goes off.
> The line between losing consciousness and falling asleep or remaining alert and in control while your physical body falls to sleep.
> A melding of thoughts from an awake traveler with a sleeping traveler.

4. Your best defense against not so nice nonphysical nasties is...
> Visualized armor or weapons.
> Bribery.
> Stay-away thoughts.
> Bad breath.

5. 'Lift-out' is...
> An elevator that does not work.
> Help from another nonphysical traveler.

> The nonphysical separation from the physical.
> An understanding of the cosmic connection.

6. Traveling beyond your body is like a puzzle because ...
> You can never find the last piece.
> You are assembling the pieces that allow you to get nonphysical.
> The hardest part to figure out is the center.
> None of the above.

7. A dream-travel may be...
> A nonphysical visit to your favorite place.
> A nonphysical travel that acts out during a dream.
> The best travel you've ever had.
> All of the above.

8. To use a desired destination as a method for traveling you would ...
> Keep a picture of the destination under your pillow.
> Choose a destination that holds a special attachment.
> Think of the destination as being in the same room with you.
> Call out to the destination.

9. The best way to sharpen your awareness while traveling is to ...
- Focus your attention on your nonphysical actions.
- Ask detailed questions.
- The first and second answers.
- The third answer.

10. When you are traveling beyond your body, thought equals ...
- Fifty percent of its weight while physical.
- The sum of all things pondered.
- Action.
- All of the above.

11. 'Vibration' is...
- A noise that disturbs your meditation.
- Bad shock absorbers on your car.
- The point at which your bed and your physical body make contact.
- A signal prior to lift-out.

12. An immediate pull-back to your physical may occur following your separation if you...
- Do not properly position your body in a N-S magnetic alignment.
- Allow random thoughts of your physical while still within close range.
- Smell your feet.
- Allow your Norjag Wave to overload.

13. You should always...
- Sit in the lotus position prior to a travel.

> Remember to open the bedroom window so your nonphysical can get outside.
> Have a basic plan for your travels.
> Tell someone where you're going.

14. Objects that are viewed nonphysically may appear to...
> Be larger than they actually are.
> Contain mass but not volume.
> Shimmer or glow.
> Move upward and downward but not sideways.

15. 'Nonverbal communication' is...
> The connection between your physical and nonphysical bodies.
> The act of unintentionally talking while you sleep.
> A rapid-fire exchange of thoughts and feelings between travelers.
> How most marriages end.

Bonus Question: What kind of doughnut did you nonverbally 'send' to me?
> Jelly with sprinkles.
> Chocolate with cream filling.
> Plain.
> Caramel topped with peanuts.

I hope you did well in the *Travel Tricks* game. I was going to give you the answers here, so that you could see how well you did, but then I realized that they are already in the book. If you feel you've done well you probably don't need to go looking for them. But if you don't feel confident in your answers you'll find that they start somewhere near the front of the book. Now you know why I was fired as a game show host.

DREAMING 101

Now that you've been primed to remember by playing the game in the previous chapter, tell me what you remember about your dream last night. Speak up, I can't hear you. You fell for that joke last time too.

Traveling beyond your body is a process that begins with the acceptance of possibilities. If you think that you can travel beyond your body you will succeed in doing so. But what if you've never looked at the possibilities? What if your night is spent primarily unconscious with nary a dream re-called? What if you are so unaware during your hours of sleep that you feel there is not one nano's chance of getting beyond your physical? And what if you asked question after question like I'm doing now? What if the questions led to more questions until at last all of the questions had been ques-tioned? And what if I really did have a point to this line of questioning? That would be really some-thing, wouldn't it?

Good morning class. Welcome to Dreaming 101. I am your teacher, Professor Guiden. It's my job to help you recall your dreams as you did when you were a free-spirited child. So please sit up straight, open your pad of paper, and choose a crayon. I'd

like you to draw a picture of the dream you remember best from last night. Try to picture all of
the wonderful events of your dream, down to the
finest detail. It's okay to remember your dreams.
There are no bad dreams. Dreams are just dreams
and can't hurt you. Dreams are friendly.

A few minutes pass and I come by your desk to
see what you've drawn. I flick the little propeller
on your beanie cap.

YOU: Here's my picture, Professor.

ME: Ah, I see that you have drawn a rocket ship
flying to the sun.

YOU: Yes, I don't remember very much. Just
something about astronauts going to the sun.

ME: So there's astronauts in there, huh? How
many were there?

YOU: There were three. And one of them was
afraid to go to the sun.

ME: Why was that?

YOU: I don't know. I guess he was afraid of
burning up.

ME: So it was a *he*. Were all the astronauts male?

YOU: Yes, they were all men.

ME: Could you see their faces?

YOU: No. And I never saw the rocket ship either.

ME: So how do you know there were men traveling to the sun as astronauts?

YOU: Because in my dream the story was all
over the news. It was a big deal because this one
astronaut made the whole ship turn around.

ME: So you saw that on the news in your
dream?

YOU: No, it was on the radio. That's right! I remember now that the perspective was from hearing the news on radio. How funny. I would never have remembered that.

ME: But you just did remember it.

YOU: Yes, I guess I did. That wasn't so hard. I'd probably remember dreams even better if I tried to.

ME: You're off to an excellent start so I'm sure you will. And while you're self-improving anyway, you should probably stop speaking as both sides of the conversation. That can't be healthy. Good thing it was only a demonstration of a dream recall method or I'd be really worried about us. I mean *you*.

The hunt-and-peck line of questioning we've just acted out works every time to pull the details from your dreams. You simply take each minor bit of information that you recall and question it so that more information comes out. Layer by layer your entire dream is recalled. You'll soon find that dreams are easier to recall because you've told yourself to do so.

As I stated, traveling beyond your body is a process that begins with the acceptance of possibilities. By recalling your dreams you tell your conscious and subconscious self that your nighty time is important time. This attention to the importance of other states of your consciousness and events is your bridge to nonphysical traveling.

Timely Advice

We all have it. Can you hear it? *Tick tock tick tock.*
That's your internal clock telling you what do to.
Wake up, get tired, go to sleep, wake up, get tired,
go to sleep. It's a shame we can't always listen to
our clocks when we're pressured by the needs of
the day. Sometimes you're awake when you'd like
to be asleep. You can't do anything about it so stop
complaining. But there are also times when you
can obey your body's clock. Those are great times,
but there's one even better time that you may not
be aware of. Your perfect time happens once a
night. During that time you feel the ease with
which your physical may drift off to sleep and
dream. But you don't have to go with it.

My perfect time is 3:41am. There are other times
when I feel inclined to drift to sleep but they are
not as intense as this one perfect time. It doesn't
matter if I've had lots of sleep or none, my physical
is ready to pass out.

Would you like to know when your perfect time
is? Speak up, I can't hear you! (I can't believe you
fell for that again.) You probably already know
when your perfect time is but don't recognize it.
While trying to overcome insomnia you probably,
quite suddenly, pass out and sleep right through
your perfect time. Shame on you for obeying your
clock. Instead, you could use this perfect time to let
your physical sleep while you duck duck goose
out of there for a while. Reaching the
awake/asleep line is much easier because you are
quickly headed there anyway.

Insomniacs may rejoice because your perfect time is easily spotted. On the next night that you think too much and toss and turn and take trips to the bathroom countless times for a change of pace and back to bed and fluff the pillow and re-adjust the blanket and drink some water and look out the window and listen to the sink drip and sigh a lot, notice the time that you finally pass out. At some point even an insomniac lets go of the reins. The relaxation wave rolls over you. Pleasant dreams.

When you stumble from bed to sit at your breakfast table, pulling yourself back awake through a cup of coffee, figure out exactly, or close to it, what time you conked out. That is your perfect time. You have about thirty minutes, starting from that perfect time, when you will be primed without much effort to get out of your physical body. You then target that time on a night you can afford to do so, which eliminates work or school nights.

Plan ahead by waking up fifteen minutes in advance of your time. Get out of bed, move around, splash cool water on your face. Don't worry about waking up too much prior to your travel attempt because, if you have targeted your time correctly, relaxation will not be a problem. As your perfect time draws near, get into bed and stay alert to your traveling plan as your physical body zooms towards sleep at a rocket's pace. You will never find a better time to travel than your perfect time. It dramatically increases your chances of reaching the awake/asleep line and lift-out. Find your time, enjoy the ride.

FASTER AND FARTHER

I'd like you to think about increasing the tension in your body. You are going to slowly bring all of your muscles together in a gentle grasp that should show no outward signs that your body is more tense than when you started. Allow a gradual and minor amount of tension so that you can feel your whole body gathered and hold it there. A pound of feathers weighs the same as a pound of nails. Lemons are this year's number one fruit. Dragonflies come in lots of colors. Are you still holding your slight amount of tension? Let it slowly go now. Even with such a gentle amount of tension being released you'll notice the welcome relief of your physical, and there's something more. You have just successfully 'loosened' your nonphysical.

As your physical tenses to your will, your nonphysical vibration speeds up a little. As you allow your physical to return to normal your nonphysical still maintains the faster speed for a few minutes. The difference in vibrational frequencies, between your nonphysical and your physical, is now farther apart. This makes it easier to slide away from your physical when you reach the awake/asleep line.

You can use this tensing method as part of your relaxation method. Tense for thirty seconds and release. Repeat three more times and rinse. By the fourth tense and release your nonphysical will be considerably 'loosened' from its close vibrational sync with your physical. Follow through with the rest of your travel plan. You'll find that your lift-out is much smoother and more controlled.

Lights Off

It's the middle of the night. It's a time for sanctuary from your long day of coping with the world. It's a time for relaxation and rejuvenation. It's a time for traveling. It's a time for... *Ack!* Turn out that light. That thing is way too bright. Excessive light hinders your relaxation, which adds an extra burden to your traveling attempt. A light source as seemingly insignificant as a glaring refrigerator bulb can upset your delicate state of relaxation. And why are you looking for something to eat at this hour anyway?

There are two remarkable inventions called a night light and a flashlight. These incredible marvels give off a more delicate glow to mimic the moonlight. These low levels of light are the perfect prelude to your traveling. You can use low light when you awaken at night or even start early before you head to bed. It's easy to do. When the sun goes down, your lights go off. Turn them all off. Let night lights and your flashlight guide you from one relaxing room to the next. Allow your internal clock to see that it's darker now and time for physical rest. You could take a relaxing shower or bath by low light. I won't peek. Then get to bed and your traveling plan.

Expectations

My longest travel was just over four hours and it was a humdinger. While there are no set rules regarding the duration of a travel I would break it down as follows, not accounting for your talent, luck, and good looks.

A first-time-ever traveler will be out for 1-2 minutes with the high side being 2-3 minutes. A traveler who has been out just a few times will average 1-5 minutes with the high side being 6-10 minutes. If you travel at least every two weeks you can expect to stay out 10-15 minutes with the high side of 16-30. If you're out once a week it's 10-30 minutes and the high side of 31-60 minutes. Beyond this point you're an expert. You're traveling every few days and your time away is only limited by physical distraction. You return when you want to and time is not a factor.

As you progress in your traveling you'll find that distance to a destination is not a hindrance. This is due to the speed at which you can move. That's not to say that if you wish to visit the next galaxy you won't be late for dinner. It's still a long way off. The amount of time it takes to reach your destination is determined by the method you choose to get there.

Distance while nonphysical is not just from here to there. It is also here to here. If you are nonphysical in your living room and increase your vibrational speed, your living room will fade and you'll find yourself in a faster vibrating nonphysical environment. The physical environment is still there but not observed by you at that moment. You can still see and feel for your physical as your desire dictates but your perception is primarily focused where you are now. Also, as I mentioned before, if you vibrate very fast the environment you reach may not even support a nonphysical body. You will be a good looking dot of consciousness.

Traveling In A Modern World

Tick Tick Tick RRRIIINNNGGGGG! The alarm brings another wonderful day. You're fresh from five hours and feeling feisty. I hope you have that out of your system now. Today will be busy. Busy, busy, busy. Your life is filled with things to do that do not allow you the time to do the things you would like to do. With so many things to do, who has the time to get out of their body? Not you, that's for sure. But I can help you by giving you a checklist for your travels. The checklist will keep you organized. And we all know that when you're organized you use your time better and you are more productive. What jerk originally said that? I want to toss a pie at him.

Your Travel Checklist

Add items of importance when you have some time.

```
1. The date was --/--/----. The time
I attempted to travel was --:--.

2. Dinner was ------. Drink was
------. Medicine / Vitamins were
------. Other: ------.
```

3. The inside temperature was --°C/F.
The humidity was high / medium / low.

4. My physical body position was
------.

5. My relaxation method was ------.

6. My travel plan of action / destination was ------.

7. It took me -- minutes to relax.

8. I noticed the following signals:
  ☐ Snoring.
  ☐ Vibration.
  ☐ Surge.
  ☐ Seeing Through My Closed Eyes.
  ☐ Pseudo Sounds / Sights.
    Describe them: ------.
  Other: ------.

9. I recall reaching the awake/asleep
line. Yes / No.

10. I traveled. Yes / No.
If No, what can you can adapt for
next time? ------.
If Yes, continue below.

11. I lifted-out in the following
manner: ------.

12. The travel occurred approximately -- minutes after I began the attempt.

13. The destination of my travel was: ------.

14. It took me – seconds / minutes to reach my destination.

15. I traveled to the destination in the following manner: ------.
(Note your nonphysical body position and actions, such as flying, running, jumping, etc.)

16. I passed through the following objects: ------.

17. I observed others while I was traveling. Yes / No.
If the answer is Yes, recall the details: ------.

18. I recall the following sights and impressions from my travel: ------.

19. I returned to the physical because I wanted to. Yes / No.
If the answer above is No, recall the details: ------.

20. My method of return to the physical was: ------.

21. After my return to the physical:
  ☐ I fell asleep and forgot the whole thing.
  ☐ I wrote an event entry in my diary.

23. I know the destination that I traveled to. Yes / No.
If the answer is Yes, detail the route taken, if possible: ------.

24. I have verified this travel by physically retracing my steps. Yes / No.

Me And You

If there is such a thing as too much of a good thing then my desire to travel nonphysically is my thing. It is my all-consuming live-it-learn-it-love-it obsession. I knew this as a child. I know this as an adult. It's my niche. But I was not born an expert and traveling was not always what I wanted to do. I wasn't always looking to get out. It took years of unintentional conditioning to get where I'm at, sitting here in an uncomfortable chair in my office. Well, not an office actually, but we've gone through that in another chapter. It was a combination of my background and a few well-timed events that sparked my obsession, so I decided to keep it.

During my childhood I found my family and friends to be of the fair-weather variety so I spent many of my hours alone. Don't cry, I'm making a point. I had lots of time all by my lonesome to think. I suppose that I could have devoted this time to my studies but that would have been too sensible. Instead, I thought about the hows whys and what-ifs. While I wasn't completely normal I wasn't too much off the mark. I was just average with a twist. So why do I tell you all of this? I'm not sure. We'll both be surprised when I get to where I'm going.

During my eighth year as me I began to wake up outside my body. It was probably my slightly odd inquisitive mentality that led to these initial events. These nonphysical events might have ceased after only a few episodes, but they didn't, because I spent lots of time alone. My lack of attentive family and friends left me with plenty of time on my hands. I spent hours experiencing and pondering and keeping it all to myself. The obsession to understand and control the event occupied my thoughts above all else until one fateful day. Yes, one amazing day *when I finally snapped out of it*. Pause for effect. Oh *please*, that day will *never* come! You must know me by now! I'm still learning new nonphysical tricks all the time. I'm still hooked. I'm still obsessed and I don't care!

My background is not all that unusual although *I* may be. This leads me to conclude that the talent to travel nonphysically is not restricted to a few individuals. I believe that anyone with a strong desire and this handbook can learn to be an expert.

While I don't encourage you to take the obsessive path that I chose, traveling does require a modicum of time and effort to accomplish. It's easier to drift into the unconsciousness of sleep than to go traveling. But if you have some time and don't mind the minor effort, you can leave your physical body just like I do. Learn the tricks, stay focused, adjust as required. Have at it, traveler! See you out there.

Alan Guiden